A gift to
Fitzgerald
Library

FROM

Arlene Hoffman

IN MEMORY OF HER HUSBAND

Raymond H. Hoffman

CLASS OF 1950

Saint Mary's
University
OF MINNESOTA

WAR AT SEA

WAR AT SEA

Modern Theory and
Ancient Practice

BY

ADMIRAL SIR REGINALD CUSTANCE

G.C.B., K.C.M.G., C.V.O., D.C.L.

WITH TWELVE PLANS AND CHARTS

CONWAY MARITIME PRESS

1970

ALL RIGHTS RESERVED

Published by Conway Maritime Press
7 Nelson Road, Greenwich, London S.E.10

by arrangement with
William Blackwood and Sons

First Edition 1918
New Impression 1970

ISBN 0 85177 012 6

Printed in Great Britain by
Lewis Reprints Limited
Port Talbot, Glamorgan

359.009

C98

Sys 3708936

IЬ05

PREFACE.

THE author has sketched the theory of war generally accepted as underlying the practice of the great leaders by sea and land in the past. As the subject has been treated at length in several works of recognised authority, an outline has seemed to be sufficient.

The wars of the ancient Greeks have been used to illustrate the theory, because the theatre of those wars being narrow, and the conditions of life comparatively simple, the working of the great drama can in each case be clearly followed. Moreover, those wars are good examples of the interdependence of the action by sea and land. Furthermore, the great struggles of Athens will probably appeal to a wider circle of readers than will any other wars, and the object of the author is to spread a knowledge of some principles underlying the conduct of war at sea. Finally, the author gladly avails himself of the opportunity to acknowledge his obligations to Dr Reginald W. Macan, D.Litt., Master of University College, Oxford, and to thank him for his valuable counsel and advice.

December 1918.

CONTENTS.

Contents.

PART II.

PELOPONNESIAN WAR.

PLANS AND CHARTS.

I.

INTRODUCTION.

In the conduct of a war are to be distinguished three influences—the political, the economic, and the military—which react on each other and tend to strengthen or weaken the national effort according as they pull in the same or in opposite directions. The connecting links between the three influences are the controlling minds—whatever be the form of Government—and public opinion, which are moved first by the political object, and later by economic necessities; then both react on the military effort. Each influence possesses a spiritual, mental, or moral as well as a material side.

The political influence depends upon the political object of the war, which may be chiefly either spiritual as in wars of religion, or material as in wars of conquest, or may combine both in various degrees. Self-interest is usually included more or less remotely—legitimately if the aim is security, illegitimately if the aim is plunder. As a general rule the more spiritual the object the more is public opinion moved, and the more intense is the resulting military effort, as has been seen when nations have fought for issues connected either with religion or with political freedom.

The economic influence is manifested in the efforts required to provide food, clothing, arms, munitions, and instruments of locomotion to carry on the war. Deficiencies in these supplies tend to weaken the military effort, not only by reducing directly the strength of the armed forces, but by impairing indirectly the spirit and *moral* both of the armed forces and of the unarmed population. The results may be either military or political, or may include both in varying degree.

The military influence finds expression in armed force, by which alone the enemy's will can be overcome and the political object attained. As between armed forces the culminating act is the fight. Hence the fight is the means through which the political object is attained; and further, the military outcome of the fight is inseparable from, and must be included in, the political object, as its chief factor.

War is a business in which battle and movement play the chief parts, and, like all other human activities, is carried on by applying means to an end. The means are men, weapons, and instruments of locomotion. Men vary indefinitely in knowledge, skill, energy, courage, and physique, whether considered as individuals or as nations, and this variation is to be found not only in different individuals and in different nations, but in the same individual and in the same nation at different times, and under different conditions. Hence in the conduct of every war the influence of man has ever been constant in its uncertainty. It is true that much concerning man's action may be learned from the part taken in past wars by commanders acting under the stress of war conditions; but war is so complex, takes place under such varying circumstances, and produces such unexpected events, that much will always be left to judgment and experience. Hence the great importance of character and ability in the leaders and their subordinates.

Weapons serve to destroy or to disarm the opponent; instruments of locomotion to move armed forces and the supplies needed by them. Hence, in the conduct of war is required some knowledge of the uses to which weapons and instruments of locomotion actually in existence can be put, and of the principles governing their use. Whether on land or sea, weapons and instruments of locomotion have changed from time to time. On land, hand weapons have been supplemented by missile weapons of ever-increasing power and efficiency, and to animal transport have been gradually added wheeled carriages, railways, motor vehicles, and aircraft. At sea, the sword and other hand weapons, the ram, the gun, the torpedo, and the mine have in turn been used; the galley of the ancients has been replaced successively by the sailing ship and the steamer, and more recently the surface ship has been supplemented by the submarine and by the aircraft. Each epoch has had its particular weapons and its typical instruments of locomotion. May it be that an examination of past wars, covering all these changes in material as well as the many phases of man's influence in the past, will reveal principles bearing on the future?

The end or military aim is primarily to destroy, or to disarm, or to neutralise the action of the enemy's armed force, whether on land, at sea, or in the air; and secondarily, to impair the resources upon which rests the strength of that force. This aim is reciprocal on either side. To destroy means to place the armed force permanently out of action; to disarm is to deprive the armed force of fighting power; if neither the one nor the other is possible, then evidently the next best thing is to neutralise its action, which can be done either by threatening to fight or by evasion. The stronger force adopts the former, the weaker one relies on the latter, but neither is more than a temporary and incomplete measure. Stress is laid on the armed force, because the decisive act in war is the battle, and because the armed force alone takes part in that decisive act. The armed force is on land an army of men, at sea a navy of ships, and in the air an aery of aircraft. Hence the primary reciprocal military aim is to destroy, or to disarm, or to neutralise the action of the army on land, the navy at sea, and the aery in the air. It is to be noted that since under modern conditions the army cannot as a rule take part in the sea battle, nor the navy in the land battle, the destruction of an army does not directly affect the balance of the navies, and *vice versa*, and therefore that the sea battle and the land battle are normally independent tactical activities. On the other hand, the aery can share in battles both by land and sea, and its destruction directly affects the balance of the armies and of the navies. Thus, the land battle and the air battle are mutually dependent tactical activities, as also are the sea battle and the air battle. Hence, the primary reciprocal military aim is to destroy, or to disarm, or to neutralise the action of the army and aery on or over the land, and the navy and aery on or over the sea.

The secondary results may be wholly or partly either political, or economic, or military. They usually follow as a consequence from the complete or partial achievement of the primary aim, since the victor can more or less do as he pleases after he has destroyed, or disarmed, or neutralised the action of the enemy's armed force. On land, he can conquer the capital and capture or evict the Government, overrun or annex territory, destroy or convert to his own use the communications and the means of production, levy contributions, and even enslave the population, thus reducing the resources of the enemy while using them to strengthen his own armed force. At sea, he can not only carry out combined naval and military operations, but can stop the movements of the merchant ships and military transports of the vanquished, while his own use of the sea is unimpeded. The stoppage of sea trade by cutting off the resources of the outside world impairs the fighting power of the vanquished, whereas the continued use of the sea enables the victor to draw wealth and supplies from foreign countries, and thus to maintain and increase his military strength. The stoppage of military transports is here included as a secondary aim, because an army embarked in transports cannot take part in battle as an organised force. Its strength as such is in abeyance until it lands.

In the air are to be found neither territory to annex nor populations to terrorise and enslave, nor means of production to utilise, nor at present any air trade to stop, whatever there may be in the future. The secondary results due to the action of the aery are at present limited to what can be achieved by reinforcing and extending the action of the army on land or of the navy at sea. In some cases these extensions may be of great importance — as, for instance, the destruction of the sources of the enemy's military strength, or the communications of an army. It is to be noted that just as sea trade can only be stopped legally outside territorial waters, so air trade, if developed, can only be stopped legally above the same sea area, because belligerent aircraft are forbidden to fly over neutral territory. It is the duty of the navy and of the aery to stop the trade of an enemy whether on the sea or in the air above it. Thus, the army and the aery have common military aims, while the navy and the aery have other common military aims. In so far as primary results alone are concerned, all battles on or over the land may be looked upon as part of one great whole, and all battles on or over the sea as part of another great whole; but when the secondary results are included, all battles, whether on land, at sea, or in air, will be seen to be part of a greater whole.

It is proposed to illustrate the theory thus sketched by examining wars at sea conducted by the ancient Greeks, confining attention to their military and economic aspects. Since the reciprocal military aim is primarily to fight, or to threaten to fight, or to evade the enemy's armed ships and aircraft, and secondarily, to stop the movements of his military transports and his trade, whether on or above the sea, it is evident that the distribution of the forces on each side should directly or indirectly aim at achieving these objects. Hence we have to consider—

1. The fight or battle.
2. The operations or movements preparatory to the fight or battle.

B

PART I.

THE CAMPAIGN OF SALAMIS.

II.

THE WEAPONS AND THE SHIPS.

In the fifth century B.C. the combatants at sea used hand weapons, such as the sword, the spear, the axe or the dagger; and missile weapons, such as the javelin or the bow, to destroy the *personnel;* the ram, to disable the ships. The hand and missile weapons were similar to those used on land; their decisive use involved close action and boarding. At that time the weapons and equipment of the different nations differed greatly, those of the Eastern nations being inferior to those of the inhabitants of Hellas. The Hellenic hoplite, whether infantryman or marine, was armed with more powerful weapons and wore more efficient protective armour, which gave him in hand-to-hand fighting a great advantage.[1]

The ram is a weapon peculiar to the sea; its effective use depends upon facility in manœuvring, which in turn hinges on speed. The higher the speed the greater is the facility in manœuvring and the probability of ramming successfully or of avoiding being rammed, since the point of the attacking ram on the one side or the attacked ship herself on the other side can be moved through a greater distance in a given small interval of time. And further, the higher the ratio between the speeds of the opponents, the greater the margin for error on the part of the faster attacking ship and the greater her corresponding advantage. This will be made clear by considering extreme cases. If one ship is at rest, the moving ship has an infinitely greater advantage, whereas if both ships are moving at equal speeds the chances of success are equal.

[1] Hdt., vii. 89 *et seq.*

It is evident that differences between ships and crews must have left room for considerable inequality between the speeds obtained.

The trireme or warship of the fifth century B.C. was about 149 feet in length and 18 feet in extreme breadth; her draught is doubtful, but may have been about 4 feet; she was usually propelled by oars, sails being fitted for use only as an auxiliary when the wind was fair. Her speed under oars was perhaps ten knots for a very short distance in fine weather, but was largely influenced by the direction and force of the wind. Her crew consisted of about 220 men, including marines, varying in number from 40, which was quite exceptional, to 10. Her sea-keeping qualities were very limited, since she was quite helpless in strong winds and was then liable to be overwhelmed by the sea. When caught in a gale on a lee shore she was usually wrecked, as happened to the Persian ships off Mount Athos in 492, and again off the coast of Magnesia and Eubœa twelve years later. Her enduring mobility was small, since the strength of the rowers was soon exhausted and the quantity of provisions and water carried was limited: Thucydides mentions that sufficient provisions for three days was embarked on a special occasion.[1] When not under way she was usually either drawn up on the beach, probably stern first, or her stern was hauled into the shore with an anchor to seaward; her crew then landed to cook their food and to sleep. It is evident that either the fleet must have been attended by a number of "victuallers" —*i.e.*, provision ships—or supplies of food must have been obtained from the country where the men landed.

Thus, the oar-propelled navies were tied to the coast by their inferior sea-keeping qualities, by their low enduring mobility, and it may be added by the difficulties of navigation in the then imperfect state of the art.

---

[1] Thu.; i. 48.

III.

THE FIGHT OR BATTLE.

SYBOTA, 432 B.C.

THE battle at sea has in the past assumed different forms, which, it is proposed to show, have been determined partly by the courage and skill of the combatants and partly by the weapons and ships in use. To this difference in form Thucydides seems to have been the first to call attention in his account of the battle off Sybota between the fleets of Corinth and Corcyra (Corfu) in the year 432 B.C. (Plan I.). His words are:—

The decks of both were crowded with heavy infantry, with archers and javelin men; for their naval arrangements were still of the old clumsy sort. The engagement was obstinate, but more courage than skill was displayed, and it had almost the appearance of a battle by land. When two ships once charged one another it was hardly possible to part company, for the throng of vessels was dense, and the hopes of victory lay chiefly in the heavy armed, who maintained a steady fight upon the decks, the ships meanwhile remaining motionless. There were no attempts to break the enemy's line. Brute force and rage made up for the want of tactics. . . .[1]

Thucydides explains that the Corinthian fleet numbered one hundred and fifty ships,—ten Elean, twelve Megarian, ten Leucadian, twenty-seven Ambraciot, one from Anactorium, and ninety of their own. The Corcyræans had one hundred and ten ships, and were supported by an Athenian squadron of ten ships, but the Athenian admiral had orders not to engage with the Corinthians unless they sailed against

[1] Thu., i. 49, Jowett's translation.

Corcyra or any place belonging to the Corcyræans and
attempted to land there. Both fleets put to sea at night with
the intention of fighting the Corinthians from Cheimerium
(Port San Giovanni) and the Corcyræans from the Sybota
islands. Both positions are on the coast of Thesprotia
(Albania) about sixteen sea miles apart, the former south-east
of the latter. On sighting one another at daybreak

they ranged themselves in order of battle. On the right (western)
Corcyræan wing were the Athenian ships. The Corcyræan ships
themselves occupied the centre and left wing, and were drawn up in
three divisions, each under the command of one of the generals.
On the right (eastern) wing of the Corinthians were the Megarian
and Ambraciot ships, in the centre the contingents of their other
allies; they themselves with their swiftest vessels formed the left
(western) wing, which was opposed to the Athenians and to the right
division of the Corcyræans.

Thus the two fleets, each probably in single [1] line abreast,
with the ships not less than two lengths apart, advanced on
wide fronts of six and seven and a half miles respectively,
and with their eastern flanks more or less covered by the
land, but with the Corcyræan western flank quite exposed
and overlapped. The presence of the Athenian squadron
and of the Corinthians themselves on the exposed flank was
a recognition of the Corcyræan's weakness there and of the
opening offered to the superior numbers of the Corinthians,
and to their overlapping fast wing division. The fleets met
and fought in the manner already described. On the eastern
wing the Corinthians suffered most. For the Corcyræans
with twenty ships routed them, drove them in disorder to
the shore and landed to plunder their encampments. On
the western wing the Corinthians had greatly the advantage
of numbers and decisively defeated the Corcyræans, whose
original inferiority was further increased by the non-return
of the twenty ships detached in pursuit. It was not until
the Corcyræans were seen to be hard pressed that the
Athenians began to take part, but by that time the battle
was decided.[2] It is evident that when two long lines of ships
are locked in equal and uncertain combat and motionless,

[1] The number of lines is not stated. Had the two sides been different in this
respect Thucydides would almost certainly have referred to it.

[2] Thu., i. 48, 49.

time is given, and an opportunity is offered, to the disengaged
ships of the more numerous fleet to double on an exposed
flank, as seems to have happened on this occasion, and to
have been the cause of the Corinthian victory.

ARTEMISIUM, 480 B.C.

In the rowing navies the weakness of the flanks was the
dominant tactical fact, and seems to have been understood
during the Greek era. Thus, during the Græco-Persian
war in the actions in the Trikeri Channel (Plan II.) north
of Eubœa (480 B.C.), the Persians, having a superiority in
numbers of at least two ships to one, attempted on two
occasions to surround the Greeks, but seemingly without
success. It is to be noted that this Channel is only four
and a half sea miles wide, and narrows to three miles at
the entrance of the Pagasæan Gulf (Gulf of Volo), and to
less than two miles on entering the Oreos Channel. On the
first day, towards the evening, the Greeks, with 271 ships
under Eurybiades the Lacedæmonian and Themistocles the
Athenian, advanced from the Artemisium strand on the north
coast of Eubœa. If the ships were at manœuvring intervals,
say two ships' lengths or one hundred yards apart, their front
would have extended 13½ miles if in one line, 6¾ miles if in two
lines, or 4½ miles if in three lines. On meeting the Persians,
who issued from an anchorage off Aphetæ on the eastern
side of the entrance to the Pagasæan Gulf, the Greeks drew
back their wings and assumed a convex formation, with
their bows out and sterns turned inwards. After an indecisive
action the approach of darkness separated the combatants,
who withdrew to their respective anchorages some ten miles
apart.[1] It has been often assumed that the Greeks formed
a complete circle. Is it not probable that this was unnecessary, since with such a long front in such narrow waters
the Greek flanks could have been covered by the land?
From the Posidium promontory to the mainland of Magnesia
is only three miles. The second day witnessed the arrival
of fifty-three triremes to reinforce the Greeks, and further
skirmishing.[2]

[1] Hdt., viii. 9-11. [2] Ibid., viii. 14.

On the third day the Greeks, having been reinforced, had 324 ships, and remained motionless off the Artemisium strand until the Persians were seen to be advancing in the formation of a half-moon, and to be seeking to encircle and to prevent the escape of the Greeks, who then moved forward to meet their assailants. The Greek front must have been longer than on the first day, and may have extended to 16, 8, or $5\frac{1}{3}$ miles, according as the ships were in one, two, or three lines. After an action in which both sides suffered considerable losses the two fleets separated. The words of Herodotus indicate that neither fleet had any clear advantage, which could not have been said if either flank of the Greeks had been doubled on.[1] Is it not probable that in this case also both flanks rested on the land? It is suggested that the Greek line probably stretched from the Posidium promontory to the Artemisium strand, which at that time may have run along the foot of the hills, forming a re-entrant angle instead of a salient. Such a line would have blocked the Oreos Channel, which the Persians sought to control. Furthermore, the Persians would have been reduced to a frontal attack, their superior numbers would have given them no advantage, and may indeed have been a hindrance, as is hinted by Herodotus, whereas the Greeks would have derived in close action full advantage from their superior weapons. A careful examination of the site can alone determine whether the coast-line has altered as is here suggested.

SALAMIS, SEPTEMBER 480 B.C.

Again, consider the battle of Salamis (Plan III.), which was fought shortly after that off Artemisium. Two days before the battle, the Greek fleet, about 375 strong, and manned by about 80,000 men under Eurybiades, the Lacedæmonian, was in and about the waters at the western entrance of the Salamis Strait, while the Persian fleet of uncertain strength but much superior in numbers—say, 600 to 700, with crews upwards of 120,000—was in Phalerum Bay and adjacent waters. The Persian king issued orders that his fleet was to fight.[2] In accordance with those orders

[1] Hdt., viii. 15, 16. [2] Ibid., viii. 69.

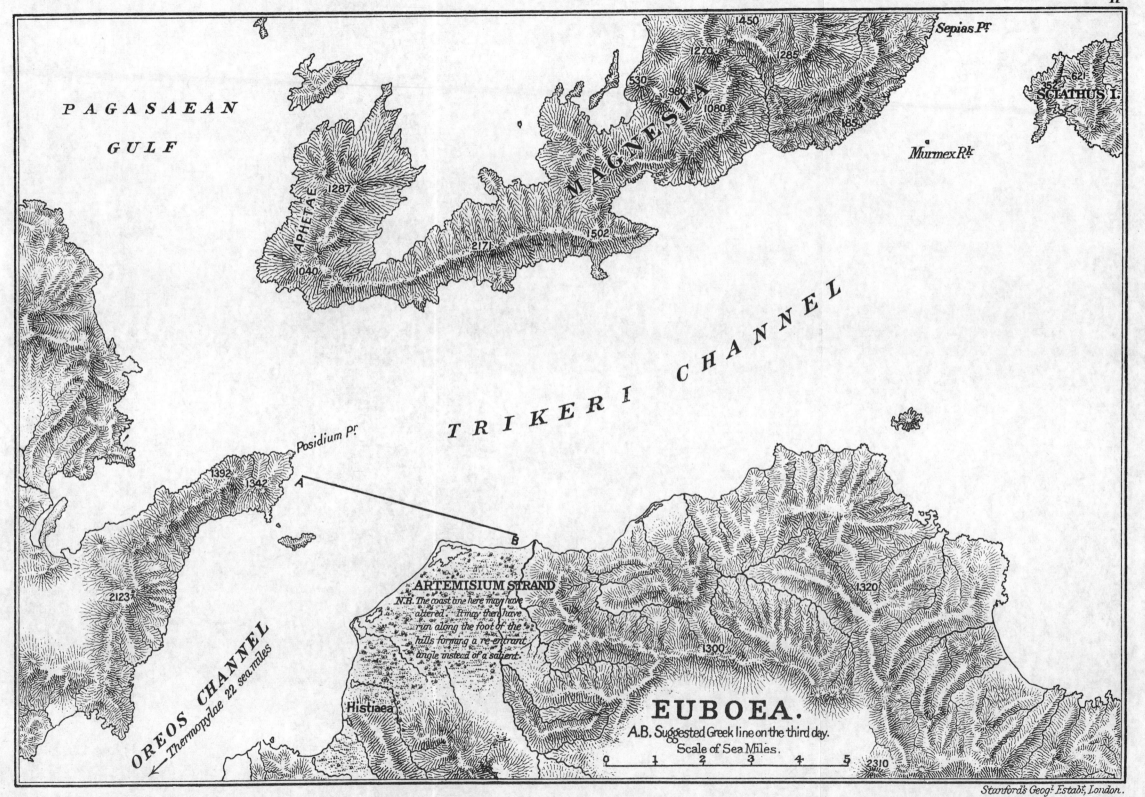

II

PAGASAEAN GULF

MAGNESIA

Sepias Pr

SCIATHUS I.

APHETAE

Murmex Rk

TRIKERI CHANNEL

Posidium Pr

OREOS CHANNEL
← Thermopylae 22 sea miles

ARTEMISIUM STRAND
N.B. The coast line here may have
altered. It may then have
run along the foot of the
hills forming a re-entrant
angle instead of a salient.

Histiaea

EUBOEA.
A.B. Suggested Greek line on the third day.
Scale of Sea Miles.
0   1   2   3   4   5

Stanford's Geogl Estabt, London.

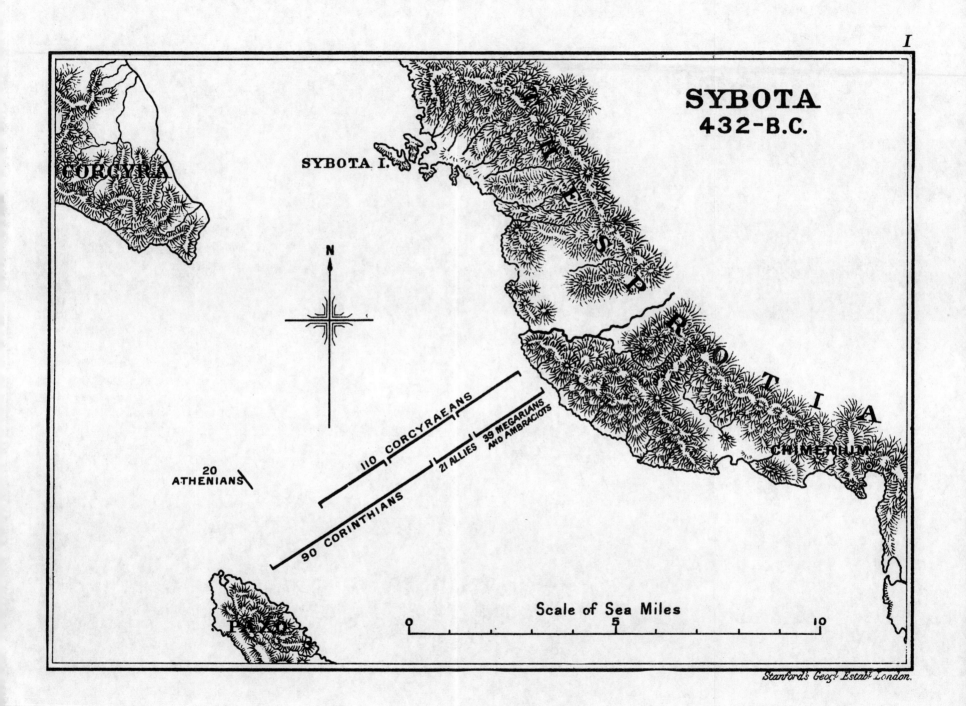

I

SYBOTA
432-B.C.

CORCYRA

SYBOTA I.

THESPROTIA

CHIMERIUM

N

110 CORCYRAEANS

21 ALLIES

39 MEGARIANS
AND AMBRACIOTS

20
ATHENIANS

90 CORINTHIANS

PAXO

Scale of Sea Miles

0   5   10

Stanford's Geogl. Establt. London.

the Persian fleet put to sea, either the day before or the night before the battle, and took station to watch the eastern passage out of the Salamis Strait and the western channel between Megaris and Salamis Island out of the Bay of Eleusis, in order to prevent the exit of the Greeks. The distance between the entrances to the two channels is about seventeen sea miles. According to Æschylus, who was a contemporary, the eastern passage was watched by a triple line of ships, by which is perhaps meant an advanced line of look-out ships backed by detachments in support and the main fleet in the open sea. The islet of Psyttaleia (Lipso), which divides the passage, was occupied by Persian troops.[1] To the western channel was sent the Egyptian squadron, originally numbering 200 ships, leaving the main fleet 400 to 500 strong.[2] Thus the Greeks were unable to put to sea without fighting.

The meagre accounts handed down to us of the battle which followed, cannot be properly understood without a knowledge of the limitations involved when handling such masses of ships and men. It has been already mentioned that the trireme, when not under way, was usually either beached or anchored with her stern hauled in to the shore. If the ships were drawn up ten yards apart, which is quite a minimum distance, the number to the sea mile would have been 200. On this basis the Greek fleet would have required nearly two miles of beach, which means not only that inside but a considerable extent of that outside Ambelaki Bay. The Persian fleet would have needed three to four miles, or considerably more than is available in Phalerum Bay. As some delay would probably occur in launching, manning, and deploying a fleet arranged at such close intervals, it seems possible that even greater stretches of beach may have been used.

If the Greek ships were at anchor, as seems possible,[3] they would have required to be not less than one ship's length apart—say fifty yards—to enable them to swing clear, but the interval may perhaps have been reduced if poles were

[1] Hdt., viii. 70, 76 ; Æschylus, *The Persians.*
[2] Diodorus, xi. 1 ; Hdt., viii. 76, 79 ; Æschylus, *The Persians.*
[3] Hdt., viii. 56, 58.

used to shove the vessels clear of each other. On that basis, if the ships were in one or more lines, their total length would have measured anything between 19 and, say, 10 miles. It is evident that the Greek fleet at anchor would have filled a considerable portion of the western end of the Strait, including Ambelaki Bay and the Georgio Channel.

The Salamis Strait is about 1600 yards wide. If the Greek fleet advanced in columns two ships' lengths—100 yards—apart, and with the same interval between the ships in column measured from stem to stem, fifteen columns would have filled the Strait, the number of ships in each column would have been twenty-five, and the length of each column about 2500 yards.

The right-hand channel leading into the eastern end of the Salamis Strait is about 1000 yards wide. If the Persian fleet advanced through it in column with a front of nine ships, as seems possible, the successive lines, after passing the narrows, would have had to wheel through an angle of about 45 degrees in order to steer up the Strait, and would then be exposed to be overlapped and outflanked at one or both ends. The left-hand channel is 800 yards wide, and would have admitted the passage of a column with a front of six ships, but the wheel after passing the narrows would have been about 135 degrees. To combine the two movements would have been extremely difficult, if not impracticable, and would have involved the risk of a Greek attack while the Persian line was in disorder. The plan shows the difficulties. In view of these, it is possible that the main advance was through the right-hand channel, while through the left-hand one was made a diversion to cover the flank. The Persian advance to attack under conditions so adverse to success may have been due either to a belief that the Greeks would not fight,[1] or to a failure to appreciate the tactical difficulties. Be that as it may, the Persians did enter the Strait in the morning, whether by one or both channels is uncertain, and appear to have been caught at a disadvantage by the Greeks, who in ordered ranks charged with their whole force, their right wing being the more advanced.[2] The result was a

---

[1] Hdt., viii. 75.   [2] Æschylus, *The Persians;* Hdt., viii. 86.

mêlée on a large scale, in which not only were the beaks or rams freely used, but ships were boarded, and hand-to-hand fights took place.[1] In short, the actual fighting was of "the old clumsy sort" to which Thucydides refers. Finally, the Persians withdrew defeated, with severe losses, to Phalerum, while the Greeks returned to Salamis. In this case it is not to be doubted that both Greek flanks were effectually covered, and that the Persians made a frontal attack. Thus was nullified the Persian superiority in numbers which would have given them an advantage on the open sea, while full scope was given to the Greek superiority in armament. The battle is one of many examples illustrating the advantage to be derived from a skilful use of the land by the inferior fleet.

[1] Hdt., viii. 88, 90.

IV.

THE OPERATIONS.

HAVING determined the form of the battle, the operations leading up to it remain to be considered.

The aim of the Persian king's invasion of Hellas in the year 480 was primarily to destroy the armed sea and land forces of the Greeks, and secondarily to overrun the country with a view to converting to Persian use all the resources, not only of Hellas, but of the then known Europe. The great enterprise was preceded by the advance into Thrace and Macedonia in 492, by the failure at Marathon two years later, and by other incidents which tend to show that it had been for several years the settled intention of the Persian autocracy. Its execution had been postponed by the Egyptian revolt, by the death of Darius, and by the disputed succession. The actual preparations, when finally renewed in 485-4, occupied four full years.[1] They included making roads and building bridges both in Asia Minor and Thrace, bridging the Hellespont, cutting a canal across the Acte (Athos) Peninsula, and collecting provisions and stores of all kinds in depôts along the route within the Persian dominions and dependencies, which then extended as far as the frontier of Thessaly. The mobilisation itself was a great undertaking. To form the fleet the whole maritime resources of the Eastern Mediterranean were laid under contribution. Ships and men were drawn from Egypt, Phœnicia, Cyprus, and the coasts of Asia Minor, including the Greek settlements in Ionia, on the islands, and on the shores of

---

[1] Hdt., vii. 20.

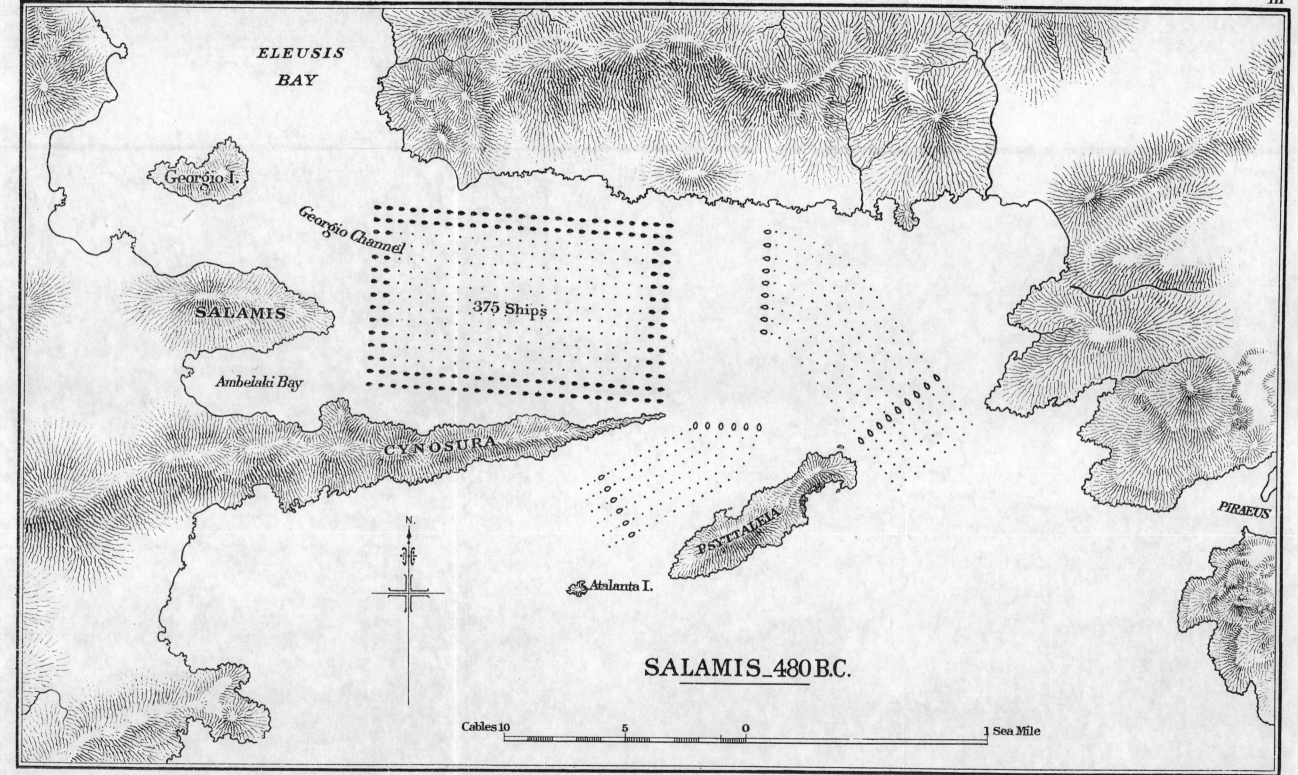

ELEUSIS
BAY

Georgio I.

Georgio Channel

SALAMIS

375 Ships

Ambelaki Bay

CYNOSURA

N.

PSYTTALEIA

PIRAEUS

Atalanta I.

SALAMIS_480 B.C.

Cables 10   5   0   1 Sea Mile

Stanford's Geogl. Estabt. London.

the Propontis and Euxine. The army was composed of contingents drawn from the many races included in the Persian empire, which then extended from the banks of the Danube and the heights of Mount Pindus to the confines of India and the southern frontier of Egypt.

The total strength of the king's forces by sea and land remains to some extent uncertain. According to Herodotus, the main fighting fleet originally consisted of some 1200 triremes, manned by about 276,000 men, including about 36,000 *epibatai* or marines; to these were added subsequently some 120 European triremes manned by about 24,000 men, so that the total line of battle strength from first to last was about 1320 triremes manned by some 300,000 men.[1] In addition to the fighting fleet proper, small craft, transports, and victuallers were provided in great numbers. Three thousand such ships manned by 240,000 men are the figures given.[2] As these auxiliary ships could not take part in the battle, their exact number is not important, but it is to be remembered that such a mass of ships must have been a serious factor in the operations, seeing that they had to be covered from attack, that anchorages had to be found for them, and that the crews had to be fed.

The figures given for the king's navy and the attendant ships seem to be large, but are not impossible, and may not be far removed from the actual strength. The numbers assigned to the army—1,700,000 infantry and 80,000 cavalry —appear to be so exaggerated that they cannot be accepted. A careful modern analysis of Herodotus' history suggests a strength more in accord with the probabilities, and leaves us with 300,000 infantry and 60,000 cavalry, accompanied by an equal number of camp-followers, say 750,000 men, as the total from Asia and Egypt, supplemented by some levies in Europe.[3]

These large forces must have taken many months to assemble. The concentration seems to have begun during the year 481,[4] as in the autumn of that year the king with a part of the army reached Sardes and wintered there.[5]

---

[1] Hdt., vii. 89, 184, 185.   [2] Ibid., vii. 184.
[3] Macan's Hdt., Books vii.-ix., vol. 2, App. 2, § 5.
[4] Hdt., vii. 26.   [5] Ibid., vii. 37.

Leaving that place on the approach of spring—say in March —he crossed the Hellespont, probably in April, and with his whole fleet and army reached Doriscus in May and Therma (Salonica) in June.

The aim of the Greeks was primarily to destroy, or to neutralise the action of, the armed sea or land forces of the Persian king, and secondarily to attain security for Hellas, its people and the Greek communities over sea. The Athenian preparations were not begun until the year 483-2, when those of the king had probably become known to the leaders in Hellas. Then began the great increase—from 50 to 200 triremes—in the Athenian navy on the initiative of Themistocles, who had for some years foreseen the Persian invasion and the need for a strong navy.[1] It was not until 481 that public opinion in Hellas became convinced of the imminence of the danger, and that an incomplete Pan-Hellenic Congress assembled at the isthmus of Corinth to consider the preparations to meet it.[2]

The Congress seems to have created a defensive league, composed the differences between the various States of Hellas, settled that Sparta should command both by land and by sea, and probably agreed on a general plan of operations. Its efforts were also directed to procure help from the Greek world outside Hellas, but without success. The Greek communities in Sicily, Italy, Corcyra, Crete, and Cyrene were in no immediate danger, whatever they might be after a victory by the king; those in Asia Minor, Thrace, and the Islands were already under the Persian yoke. The Greek leaders had to rely on forces drawn from Hellas alone, but Thessaly and Northern Greece were much exposed, and Central Greece was also liable to be overrun by the invading army, so that their inhabitants might be compelled to join the enemy. Thus the available force was liable to reduction if the invasion were not stayed on the frontiers of Thessaly.[3] The potential strength, if all Hellas had taken part and remained firm, is not known, but some idea of it can be deduced from the ultimate numbers of the fleet at Salamis, which were about 375 triremes, and of the army the following year at Platæa, which have been estimated as 110,000 fighting men; but

---

[1] Thu., i. 14; Hdt., vii. 144. [2] Ibid., vii. 145. [3] Hdt., vii. 172.

among this number must probably be included part of the crews of the fleet which had been by that time reduced to 110 triremes.[1] It will be seen that the king's fleet and army probably outnumbered those of the Greeks by more than two to one, but as has been already pointed out, their quality was inferior owing to their indifferent armament and equipment.

The reciprocal problem was, with fleets and armies superior on the one side in numbers and on the other side in arma-ment and equipment—*i.e.*, in the quality of the units—to fight battles at sea and on land in positions where victories could as far as possible be assured, that is to say, under the most favourable tactical conditions. In other words, the king should have aimed at conditions favourable to numbers, the Greeks at those which give advantage to superior armament. But we are to note that whereas difference in numbers is a tangible thing and readily appreciated, difference in quality, until actually tested, is usually not recognised by those who have not adopted an improved armament. Notwithstanding the large war experience of the Persian leaders during the preceding fifty years, the king and his advisers may have made this mistake. Furthermore, the fleet and army were closely interdependent. The fleet covered or threatened, as the case may be, the sea-borne supplies of both services, then of great importance to the king, as the local supplies of Hellas, which was then, as it is now, largely dependent on imported food, cannot have been equal to the demands of such masses of men. Moreover, land transport was limited. Similarly, the army covered, or threatened, the harbours and landing-places, then so necessary to the fleets, owing to their inferior sea-keeping qualities and low enduring mobility. Again, the fleet also covered the flank and rear of its own army, or threatened those of the enemy, but the danger of the flank being turned from the sea was more especially applicable to the Greeks. Thus, the strategical interdepen-dence of the sea battle and the land battle was then, as it has been ever since, and is now, very considerable. A victory or defeat at sea reacted more or less on the operations on land, and *vice versa*. It follows that the positions selected for the battles at sea were probably governed not only by the

[1] Hdt., viii. 131.

C

requirements of the battle, but also to some extent by the movements of the army. Bearing these considerations in mind the actual operations can be set forth.

At some uncertain time during the spring of the year 480 envoys from Thessaly requested the Greeks to send troops to occupy the defile of Tempe—the easiest route from Macedonia into Thessaly. In accordance with that request a force of about 10,000 heavy armed infantry under Evænetus the Spartan, and Themistocles the Athenian, was sent by sea, landed in the Pagasæan Gulf (Gulf of Volo), occupied the pass, and was joined there by Thessalian cavalry. In a few days the leaders seem to have realised that their position could be turned by an enemy advancing over the mountains —probably through Oloosson (Elassona)—and that reliable troops were not available in sufficient numbers to hold such an advanced position against a much more numerous enemy. The detachment withdrew, re-embarked and returned home.[1] Later on Thessaly threw in her lot with and fought for the king.[2]

After withdrawing from Thessaly the Greeks determined to make a stand at sea in the Trikeri Channel north of Eubœa and on land at Thermopylæ, but they did not occupy those positions until the Persian army advanced from Therma into Pieria (Olympus)—say in July.[3] Then they moved forward a fleet under Eurybiades and Themistocles to the Artemisium strand on the north coast of Eubœa, and a detachment of the army under Leonidas, the Spartan king, to Thermopylæ.[4] The position selected for the fleet was well chosen. Its base on the island of Eubœa was immune from attack by the Persian army. The narrow waters of the Eubœan channel were tactically favourable to the less numerous but better armed Greek fleet. The Persian fleet could not pass without a battle, seeing that a movement outside Eubœa would expose not only the convoy to attack but the whole fleet to the risk of navigating the open sea and of being caught on an iron-bound lee shore, without shelter from easterly winds, for a distance of about eighty sea miles. The flank of the Greek army at Thermopylæ was covered. The strength of the fleet left much to be desired, as it originally

[1] Hdt., vii. 172, 173. [2] Ibid., vii. 174. [3] Ibid., vii. 175. [4] Ibid., vii. 177.

numbered only 271, although subsequently reinforced to 324, as against its full strength 375 at Salamis. If a decision was to be sought in the Trikeri Channel every effort should have been made to be there in full strength.

The Thermopylæ position was then a narrow pass between the mountains and the sea, suitable for defence so long as the mountain passes were held and the fleet was undefeated and remained in those waters. The strength of the detachment under Leonidas is uncertain, but is believed to have been anything between 8000 and 12,000 men all told. Such a force was far too weak for the work to be done, and could not be expected to reach a favourable decision. It might temporarily hold up, but could not hope to defeat the greatly superior numbers of the king.

The king's fleet remained at Therma until his army, after traversing Thessaly, reached the approaches to Thermopylæ —say in August—when it put to sea, the waters as far as Sciathus being previously reconnoitred by a fast detachment which came in contact with Greek look-out ships.[1] Sailing probably at early dawn and favoured by the weather, the fighting fleet reached the neighbourhood of Cape Sepias, distant some eighty sea miles, the same evening, and anchored along the shore in eight lines,[2] which would have stretched nearly four or eight sea miles, according as the ships were one or two ships' lengths apart. But we are to remember that there was a very numerous convoy of ships, probably largely dependent upon sail power, and therefore unable to make much headway in light airs. These could not have reached so far, and must have either anchored more to the northward or remained under weigh throughout the night.[3] In the morning an easterly gale came on suddenly, and lasted three days, during which the fleet was in a most hazardous position on a lee shore. According to Herodotus, the losses were four hundred triremes, besides a great number of the convoy, the coast from the Sepias Promontory to Melibœa under Mount Ossa, a distance of about forty sea miles, being strewn with their wrecks.[4]

Either before or during the same gale the Greek fleet seems

[1] Hdt., vii. 179. [2] Ibid., vii. 183, 188.
[3] Ibid., vii. 188. [4] Ibid., vii. 188, 190, 191.

to have been withdrawn through the Oreos Channel from their exposed position on the Artemisium strand, and to have sought security or shelter under the lee of Eubœa. On the morning of the fifth day—the day of sailing from Therma being reckoned as the first—the king's fleet again put to sea, the gale having moderated during the night, and proceeded to Aphetæ, a position at the entrance to the Pagasæan Gulf.[1] It is necessary to note that on some uncertain date the king detached a squadron of some two hundred triremes to pass round outside Eubœa for the purpose either of intercepting the retreat of the Greeks through the Euripus between Eubœa and the mainland, or of threatening the position at Thermopylæ.[2] This detachment seems to have been caught either in the same or in a different gale, and nearly all the ships appear to have been wrecked.[3] Such were among the risks which limited the movements of ships and fleets throughout the rowing era. The movements of the Greek fleet during the three days' gale are somewhat uncertain, but on the same fifth day it was again on the Artemisium strand. The two fleets were now in presence and some ten sea miles apart.[4]

Although the figures of Herodotus may not be strictly accurate, it seems highly probable that the King's fleet was still at least twice as numerous as that of the Greeks, even after allowing that the detached ships were absent from the engagements on the afternoon of the fifth and two following days, as already described.[5] It is, however, not to be doubted that the serious losses due to the storm had a disorganising and depressing effect on the officers and men of the king's fleet and a correspondingly encouraging influence on the Greek personnel. This may be the reason why the king's fleet awaited attack on the first two days, and did not take the initiative until the third day. Be that as it may, the actions at sea were indecisive.

Turning to the operations on land, it will be remembered that on the first day of the movement of the fleet from Therma the king's army was in front of Thermopylæ.[6] It remained inactive during the three following days of the

---

[1] Hdt., vii. 193. [2] Ibid., viii. 7. [3] Ibid., viii. 13, 14.
[4] Ibid., viii. 4. [5] Cp. p. 13 *supra*. [6] Cp. p. 23 *supra*.

gale. On the fifth day, when his fleet moved to Aphetæ, the king began his attack at Thermopylæ, renewed it on the sixth day without success, and turned the Greek position on the seventh day. Thus the three actions fought on land synchronised with those at sea.[1] The Greek army, its position having been turned, was forced to retreat with loss, including the total destruction of the rearguard under Leonidas. The Peloponnesian survivors withdrew to the Isthmus of Corinth where their army was assembling. The central states, except Phocis, abandoned the cause of Hellas and joined the king, who was now free to overrun Attica and to advance to Athens, then unwalled and defenceless, since nearly all its men were in the fleet.

The night following the defeat at Thermopylæ and the indecisive action at sea the Greek fleet withdrew south inside Eubœa.[2] The leaders were doubtless unwilling to risk another action in the Trikeri Channel, and were aware that their retreat through the narrow Euripus was threatened. Moreover, the army no longer needed their support in Eubœan waters. And further, there may already have arisen doubts whether the Peloponnesian army would be moved forward to cover Bœotia and Attica, as seems to have been previously arranged.[3] Leaving the Artemisium strand on the night of the seventh day, Salamis, distant about one hundred and sixty sea miles, was probably reached not later than the morning of the tenth day. On arrival the leaders found that the Peloponnesian army was still at the Isthmus, where it remained during the subsequent operations. The inhabitants of Athens were now moved to the island of Salamis, to Ægina, and to Trœzen.[4] The Greek fleet was further reinforced and took up a position in Salamis Strait.[5] Some uncertain number of days later the king's army reached and occupied Athens, and his fleet presently arrived in Phalerum Bay.[6] But this occupation was no decision. It was not Athens but the armed Athenians who resisted, and they had gone elsewhere. The two fleets were again in presence, but owing to reinforcements on the one side and to losses on the other, the king's superiority in numbers does

---

[1] Hdt., viii. 15. [2] Ibid., viii. 18, 21, 22. [3] Ibid., viii. 40.
[4] Ibid., viii. 41. [5] Ibid., viii. 42. [6] Ibid., viii. 50, 66.

not seem at this time to have much exceeded fifty per cent. The position taken up by the Greek fleet in Salamis Strait was justified for the same sound tactical and strategical reasons as was that in the channel north of Eubœa. As Themistocles is said to have pointed out, not only did its narrow waters condition victory, but the fleet there covered directly the refugees on Salamis island and indirectly the Peloponnesian army at the Isthmus.[1] The king's army might advance there, but after the experience at Thermopylæ success in a frontal attack may have seemed doubtful, and without the fleet the Greek position could not be turned. If the king's army were held up, it could not remain there for any length of time without sea-borne supplies, and these might not be forthcoming. Before the king's fleet could pass to the Isthmus either the Greek fleet must be destroyed or a force must be left to neutralise its action, since the all-important sea supplies might otherwise be cut off. This means that if the king's advance was to be continued, his fleet must either divide or fight. To divide the fleet would probably have compromised the numerical superiority on which reliance was placed.[2] He decided to fight. Themis-

---

[1] " With thee it rests, O Eurybiades ! to save Greece, if thou wilt only hearken unto me, and give the enemy battle here, rather than yield to the advice of those among us, who would have the fleet withdrawn to the Isthmus. Hear now, I beseech thee, and judge between the two courses. At the Isthmus thou wilt fight in an open sea, which is greatly to our disadvantage, since our ships are heavier and fewer in number than the enemy's, and further, thou wilt in any case lose Salamis, Megara, and Ægina, even if all the rest goes well with us. The land and sea force of the Persians will advance together ; and thy retreat will but draw them towards the Peloponnese, and so bring all Greece into peril. If, on the other hand, thou doest as I advise, these are the advantages which thou wilt so secure ; in the first place, as we shall fight in a narrow sea with few ships against many, if the war follows the common course, we shall gain a great victory ; for to fight in a narrow space is favourable to us—in an open sea, to them. Again, Salamis will in this case be preserved, where we have placed our wives and children. Nay, that very point by which ye set most store is secured as much by this course as by the other ; for whether we fight here or at the Isthmus, we shall equally give battle in defence of the Peloponnese. Assuredly ye will not do wisely to draw the Persians upon that region. For if things turn out as I anticipate, and we beat them by sea, then we shall have kept your Isthmus free from the barbarians, and they will have advanced no further than Attica, but from thence have fled back in disorder ; and we shall, moreover, have saved Megara, Ægina, and Salamis itself, where an oracle has said that we are to overcome our enemies. . . ."—*Rawlinson's Herodotus*, vol. iv. p. 253.

[2] Cp. Hdt., vii. 236.

tocles had forced a battle on the king, and had selected the site. The battle took place on or about 20th September, and resulted in the defeat of the king, as has been already explained. The principle, put into practice at Salamis, of limiting the movements of a hostile fleet by taking up a position flanking its advance is of first-rate importance, and has been often [1] applied since that battle.

During the night following the battle, or perhaps later, the remnant of the defeated fleet retreated to the Hellespont.[2] Doubtless the attendant transports and supply ships also left the waters of Hellas. After an interval of uncertain duration —due possibly to the need to cover the refugees on Salamis from attack by the king's army—the Greek fleet followed in pursuit, but their exertions seem to have been belated and abortive. It is true their advance threatened the king's communications across the Hellespont, but they did not proceed beyond Andros,[3] being probably held back by the risk of crossing the long stretch of open sea beyond, by difficulties of supply and by the then difficulties and uncertainty attending operations on coasts controlled by an enemy. They were content to lay siege to Andros, in which they were not successful, and to raid Carystus in Eubœa. They also seem to have taken other steps to bring under Hellenic control those islands of the Cyclades group which had embraced the cause of the Persians.[4] The reader will observe that in those days, when fleets were tied to the coast by their low enduring mobility, these islands were important stepping-stones across the Ægean. Finally, the fleet retired to Salamis and the campaign at sea ended for that year. Meanwhile the refugees had returned from Salamis to Athens.

The Greek fleet had achieved its primary aim, and for more than half a century no Persian fleet reappeared in Hellenic waters. The secondary results followed as a consequence. The king's sea-borne military supplies were stopped, and thus were limited the movements of his army, which, threatened with the difficulty of subsistence in Attica,

---

[1] Cf. Armada Campaign, 1588 ; Togo, off Port Arthur, 1904 ; and in the Straits of Tsu Sima, 1905.

[2] Hdt., viii. 107.   [3] Ibid., viii. 108.   [4] Ibid., viii. 111, 112.

was withdrawn into Thessaly.[1] Eventually Mardonius was
left with a select part of the army to complete the conquest
of Hellas, while the king with the remainder retreated with
loss through Thrace and crossed over into Asia.[2] It will be
noted that the retirement was brought about by the action
of the Greek fleet alone, since the Peloponnesian army at the
Isthmus, covered by the fleet from attack, did not move.
More than that, the fleet could not achieve. Its victory
had been decisive at sea. To eject Mardonius and his army
from Europe a similar decision was required on land, which
could be brought about more quickly and more effectively by
the direct action of an army than by any indirect action of
a fleet. The reciprocal action of armies and fleets is nearly
always indirect, and is usually seen in the secondary results
achieved.

During the winter no movements of importance took place
on either side by land or sea. The Persian fleet was at
Cymè—a port on the mainland about twenty miles south-
east of Lesbos—and at Samos;[3] the army of Mardonius was
in Thessaly and Macedonia[4] with outlying detachments,
perhaps in northern and central Greece; the Greek fleet
and army remained at home. On the approach of spring—
say in March—the Persian fleet mustered at Samos 300
strong under Mardontes and remained there;[5] the Greek
fleet assembled at Ægina to the number of 110 under the
command of Leotychides the Spartan and Xanthippus the
Athenian,[6] but in response to pressing entreaties for help
from Ionia presently moved to Delos.[7] Thus the two fleets
faced each other at either end of the safest and best route
across the Ægean offered to triremes under the lee of Icaria.

Seemingly about the time when the fleets began to re-
assemble, embassies reached Athens both from Mardonius
and from Sparta. The former made offers to induce Athens
to abandon the cause of Hellas; the latter as a counter-
proposal offered an asylum to the inhabitants of Attica during
the war. Athens rejected both offers, remained firm for
resistance to the Persian, declined to withdraw to the

---

[1] Hdt., viii. 113.   [2] Ibid., viii. 115, 117.   [3] Ibid., viii. 130.
[4] Ibid., viii. 126.   [5] Ibid., viii. 130.   [6] Ibid., viii. 131.
[7] Ibid., viii. 132, 133.

Peloponnesus, and pressed that the army should be moved forward from the Isthmus into Bœotia, and there, united with the Athenians, give battle to the enemy.[1]

Shortly after the rejection of his offer Mardonius, intent on re-occupying Athens, began to advance.[2] As soon as he reached Bœotia, and it was seen that the Peloponnesian army was not to advance but to remain inactive at the Isthmus, the inhabitants of Athens again moved either to Salamis or on board the ships required to cover that island.[3] Presently Attica was overrun and Athens occupied for the second time some ten months after the first—say in June.[4] Meanwhile Athenian envoys were sent to Sparta again to urge the advance of the army. Safely covered by the Athenian fleet, and possibly in doubt about the attitude not only of Argos and other neighbours, but of her own helot population, Sparta procrastinated, but finally came to see that if that fleet changed sides the Peloponnesus would no longer be safe. Orders were given for the advance of the army.[5] Whereupon Mardonius at once evacuated Attica— say in July—and withdrew into Bœotia,[6] where some two months later—say in August or September—his total defeat at Platæa finally freed Hellas and Europe from the autocratic rule of the Persian king.

As soon as Attica was evacuated the refugees in Salamis were free to return to Athens, and the covering ships were no longer tied to home waters; but whether any reinforcement was sent to the fleet is not known. However that may have been, Leotychides and Xanthippus, in response to a renewed invitation, advanced to Samos.[7] The strength of the two fleets now face to face is not exactly known, but weakened by the absence of the Phœnician squadron, and probably distrusting the Ionian Greek division, Mardontes refused battle, withdrew to the mainland, beached his ships near Priene, and threw up defences around them.[8] The Greeks followed. Notwithstanding the presence of a considerable Persian army near by at Mycale, they disembarked, stormed the Persian defences, burned the ships, and then

[1] Hdt., viii. 140-144.   [2] Ibid., ix. 1.   [3] Ibid., ix. 6.
[4] Ibid., ix. 3.   [5] Ibid., ix. 9-11.   [6] Ibid., ix. 15.
[7] Ibid., ix. 90, 96.   [8] Ibid., ix. 97.

re-embarked.[1]   The battle at Mycale was fought about the same time as that at Platæa, and completed the work begun at Salamis.   The Greek fleet being supreme in the Ægean, now proceeded to Abydus in the Hellespont, whence Leoty-chides and the Peloponnesian ships returned home.   Xanthippus with the Athenian division crossed the Hellespont and laid siege to Sestus.   The capture of that place gave them control of the Thracian Chersonese (Gallipoli Peninsula) and of the crossing between Europe and Asia.[2]

The Greeks had succeeded in their primary military aims. The armed forces of the king both by land and sea had been defeated and destroyed.   The inferiority of the Asiatic to the Greek as a fighting man had been made manifest.   As a consequence the invasion of Europe by Asia was stopped and security was assured for a long period.   The victory at sea produced great results on Hellas itself.   It laid the foundation of the Delian league and of the naval supremacy of Athens, which ultimately led to the Peloponnesian War.

[1] Hdt., ix. 99-106.   [2] Ibid., ix. 114, 118.

PART II.

THE PELOPONNESIAN WAR.

V.

THE WEAPONS AND THE SHIPS.

AT the outbreak of the Peloponnesian war in 431, the weapons and the ships seem to have been substantially similar to those in use during the campaign of Salamis. It is true that during the intervening half century changes are said to have been introduced in the ships to give room on their decks for a larger number of fighting men,[1] and therefore favourable to hand-to-hand fighting. But these changes were either not permanent, or, if permanent, were not turned to account during the war, seeing that the number of fighting men carried was reduced to meet the change introduced in the form of the battle, as will be explained. No important changes in weapons or ships are known to have been made during the war until the nineteenth year, when the Corinthians made use of ships with strengthened beaks which gave then an advantage in a stem-to-stem charge.[2]

---

[1] Plutarch ; Cimon.   [2] Thu., viii. 34.

VI.

THE FIGHT OR BATTLE.

IT has been seen that the system of fighting off Sybota in the year 433-2 was the same as that at Salamis nearly half a century earlier. The first engagement at sea during the Peloponnesian war occurred in the year 429, and indicated a great change. The form or order of battle was no longer the same. Before describing the "new system" it will be instructive to call attention to the probable causes of the change.

The formation of the Hellenic Maritime Confederacy, known as the Delian League, in the year 478, gave to Athens sooner or later a fixed income, since she acquired complete executive control over the money contributed by the Confederates.[1] With this money came to be maintained a standing professional Athenian Navy, with an improved equipment and with well-paid crews of freemen, who were kept in constant practice by the frequent wars of the period. The result was a skilled body of seamen, who propelled their ships at higher speeds and manœuvred them with greater skill than did those of other states. The professional pride of the seaman in handling his ship finally led him to trust to his skill as a seaman rather than as a soldier. He was led to trust to manœuvring rather than to fighting hand to hand, and adopted as a weapon the ram in addition to the sword and other hand or missile weapons. The descriptions of the earlier battles of the war given by Thucydides show that the adoption of the ram and the reliance on manœuvring brought

[1] Thu., i. 96 ; v. 18 ; vii. 28.

about the substitution of the line ahead for the line abreast as the Athenian order of battle. But this did not last. The later battles show that the line abreast again came into use after the superiority in speed had been lost.

PHORMIO AND MACHAÔN OFF NAUPACTUS, 429 B.C.

The first recorded instance of "the new system" occurred off Naupactus in the year 429 (Plan IV.). The facts as to the first engagement are that an Athenian squadron of twenty ships under Phormio was lying at anchor near the entrance to the Gulf of Corinth. A Peloponnesian squadron under Machaôn of forty-seven ships, carrying troops and not equipped for action, passed out of the Gulf hugging the southern shore. Phormio, keeping along the northern shore, followed Machaôn's movements, and forced an action in the open sea, when Machaôn attempted to cross the channel during the early morning calm usual in those waters. When threatened with attack Machaôn assumed a defensive attitude, and formed his ships in the largest possible circle without leaving space to break through, turning their bows out and their sterns inwards. Within the circle were placed the smaller craft and five of the fastest ships, which latter were to move to any point attacked. Phormio with his ships in single line ahead did not attack at once, but threatened to do so by steering quite close round and round Machaôn's ships. This threat gradually crowded the Peloponnesian ships into a narrower and narrower space, so that when the usual sea breeze sprang up, not having room to work their oars, they fell into confusion. Then Phormio made the signal to charge, and won a complete victory.[1]

We are to note that the line ahead is a formation favourable not only to manœuvring, but also to the use of the ram as a weapon, since each ship is covered by its next astern; and further, that Phormio's ships moving at speed were under full command, and therefore had a great advantage over their opponents, who were lying motionless without any room to get weigh on, and thus to improve their chances with

---

[1] Thu., ii. 83, 84.

the ram. The circular formation made counter-attack impossible, owing to lack of speed, and defence weak, in that the ships did not cover each other from the ram attack.

NICOSTRATUS AND ALCIDAS OFF CORCYRA, 427 B.C.

That the circular formation off Naupactus was due to the fear of being outflanked and doubled upon, is shown by the action off Corcyra two years later (Plan V.). On the day preceding the action a Peloponnesian squadron of fifty-three triremes under Alcidas anchored for the night at Sybota, distant some eighteen sea miles from the city of Corcyra, where was lying an Athenian squadron of twelve triremes under Nicostratus. At daybreak Alcidas proceeded for Corcyra. Sixty hastily-manned Corcyræan triremes straggled out in disorder to meet him. Against these he detached twenty ships, and with the remaining thirty-three advanced to meet the twelve Athenians. Thucydides tells us that "the Athenians, afraid of being surrounded by superior numbers, did not attack the centre of those opposed to them, but fell upon the wings and sank a single ship; then, the enemy forming in a circle, they rowed round them and endeavoured to throw them into confusion."[1]

There is nothing to show that the two wings were attacked at the same time, or that Nicostratus divided his small force. It is probable that he did not make such a mistake, but that with his whole force he turned one wing and then the other. We are to picture the thirty-three Lacedæmonians advancing in single line abreast on a front extending upwards of three thousand yards, and the twelve Athenians in single line ahead moving at higher speed, perhaps obliquely across their front, to outflank them. A long line cannot change front readily, and therefore, to prevent the wing—say the right—being turned and enveloped and the rear then threatened, the ships on that wing would turn outwards into single line[2] and be gradually headed off by the faster squadron; those in the centre and on the further wing would either follow or, uncertain what to do, would perhaps stop

[1] Thu., iii. 78. [2] Cf. Cynossema, 411 B.C., and Lepanto, 1571 A.D.

IV

Phormio and Machaon off
NAUPACTUS
First Action _ 4.29 B.C.

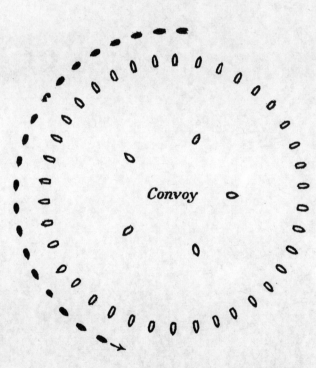

Convoy

500   0   500   1000   1500 Yards.

rowing until threatened in their turn from the rear by the encircling enemy. Finally, we are to see the whole fleet rounded up in a circle with the Athenians rowing round them as at Naupactus. Alcidas was only saved from a repetition of that defeat by the return of the twenty ships detached. Their arrival compelled Nicostratus to withdraw. The picture thus drawn depicts the possible and the probable, but whether it correctly represents the actual facts can never be known for certain. The assumed Athenian tactics are similar in principle to those of the Japanese in the action with the Chinese off the Yalu in September 1904.[1]

The successes of Phormio off Naupactus and of Nicostratus off Corcyra were due to superior mobility. The speeds attained by the well-trained Athenian standing crews may have exceeded those reached by the unpractised Peloponnesian levies in the ratio of five to four—say two knots. This high-speed ratio made the ram more effective, but hand weapons were sacrificed in that the number of *epibatai* or marines carried was reduced, which weakened the Athenians when hand-to-hand fighting was forced on them. Here is seen the earliest example of the rival demands of fighting power and speed. Furthermore, the flexible line ahead gave better manœuvring power against the rigid line abreast, and the high-speed ratio, coupled with the short distance between the fleets, made the "rounding up" of the slow fleet easy, although the absolute speeds were low. In fact, Phormio and Nicostratus proved that against superior numbers the ram as a weapon, coupled with higher mobility, gave as great an advantage in the open sea as was given by superior hand weapons alone in the narrow waters of Salamis. It is important to note that this result was attained by skill in manœuvring a fleet and not in handling a single ship—*i.e.*, in ramming, as has usually been assumed.

Phormio and Cnemus off Naupactus, 429 b.c.

But the new system had its limitations, as was shown by the second engagement off Naupactus, which occurred shortly

[1] 'The Ship of the Line in Battle,' p. 91, by the Author.

D

after the first.[1] (Plan VI.) In this case Phormio, with the
same twenty triremes, was lying on the north shore just
outside the entrance to the Gulf of Corinth, as he wished
to fight in the open sea.[2] Cnemus with seventy-seven
Peloponnesian ships arrived and anchored on the south
shore inside the Gulf, not far from Panormus, where the
Peloponnesian army was co-operating with him. The two
fleets seem to have been three to four sea miles apart. The
Narrows are about one sea mile wide.

The Peloponnesian plan was to draw the Athenians inside
the Gulf, then to pen them against the land, and thus to
neutralise their superior mobility. With this object in view
Cnemus weighed in the early morning to threaten an attack
on Naupactus, the undefended base held for the Athenians by
their allies the Messenians. That town lies inside the Gulf and
distant four to five sea miles from the Narrows. When Cnemus
moved, Phormio immediately embarked, passed the Narrows
and stood along the northern shore to cover Naupactus.
Cnemus had his fleet in four line ahead columns, disposed
abeam, with nineteen to twenty ships in each and the fastest
ships leading. Phormio was in single line ahead. As the
ships in column cannot have been less than two ships'
length—one hundred yards—apart from stem to stem—*i.e.*,
one ship's length between them—the columns in each fleet
must have stretched at least one sea mile. The reader
is asked to visualise the two fleets steering more or less
parallel courses; the Peloponnesian the more advanced; the
Athenians gradually coming up and having the land half a
mile or less to port. Finally, when the Athenian van had
advanced, but was still abaft his centre, Cnemus made
the signal to turn together eight points—90 degrees—to
port, bore down in four lines abreast, disposed astern,
and cut off the nine rear Athenian ships, driving them on
shore, where they were succoured by the Messenian army.
The eleven triremes in the van pulled hard for Naupactus,
where, heads to seaward, they prepared to resist attack. The
Peloponnesian fast division pursued, but their leading ship
having been rammed and sunk by the rearmost Athenian,
they stopped and fell into disorder. Whereupon the Athenians

[1] Thu., ii. 86-92.   [2] Ibid., ii. 89.

V

Nicostratus and Alcidas off
CORCYRA _ 427 B.C.

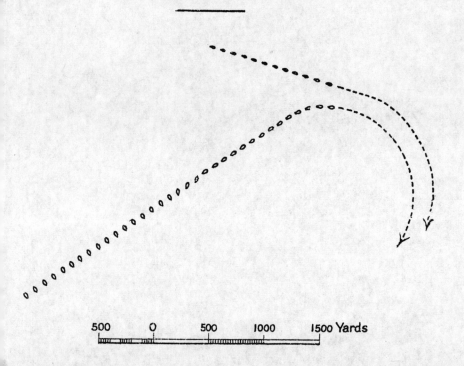

500   0   500   1000   1500 Yards

again attacked and defeated them with loss. The Peloponnesians fled to Panormus, and sought shelter under the protection of their army at that place.

We are to note the failure of Phormio to force a battle in the open sea; also the tactical use of the land by Cnemus, and the steps taken by him to neutralise superior speed and prevent encircling by assuming in advance a position on the bow of the enemy, by placing his fastest ships in the van, and by decreasing the length and increasing the depth of his fleet. That it is not always possible to bring on a battle in the open sea against the enemy's will was again shown four years later 425, at Pylus. There the fighting, as will be seen, was of the "old clumsy sort" and skill in manœuvring in the open sea did not find its opportunity.

DIPHILUS AND POLYANTHES OFF ERINEUS, 413 B.C.

The next battle at sea requiring attention is that in which the strengthened Corinthian beaks were first used. It was fought in the same waters as those in which Phormio had employed "the new system" sixteen years before. An Athenian squadron of thirty-three ships under command of Diphilus was at Naupactus. A Peloponnesian squadron of nearly the same number, commanded by Polyanthes the Corinthian, lay some nine miles to the eastward at Erineus in a crescent-shaped bay on the southern shore of the Gulf of Corinth. Polyanthes had anchored his ships in a close single line, with his flanks resting on the projecting promontories, which were held by detachments of the army co-operating with him.[1] Thus, only a frontal attack on him was possible. The Athenians put to sea and advanced towards the Peloponnesians, but seem to have hesitated to attack. After an interval of uncertain duration Polyanthes made the signal to charge. Details of the battle are wanting. We are only told that three Corinthian ships were destroyed and seven Athenian ships were disabled by frontal blows with the stronger beaks.[2] It is to be noted that whereas Phormio's

[1] Cf. Barrington at St Lucia, 1779, and Hood at St Kitts, 1782.
[2] Thu., vii. 34.

victories were won over superior numbers, the results were indecisive in this battle between equal numbers. The difference was due not alone to the strengthened rams, but rather to the skilful use of the land by which the Peloponnesians avoided a battle in the open sea, and neutralised any possible superior Athenian speed and skill.

THRASYLLUS AND MINDARUS AT CYNOSSEMA, 411 B.C.

The first battle at sea on a large scale after the destruction of the Athenian navy at Syracuse was fought in the Hellespont during the Ionian war about August 411, and is known as the battle of Cynossema (Plan VII.). No longer were the Athenian crews superior to those in other navies and able to propel their ships at higher speeds. The essential facts in connection with the battle were as follows [1] :—

The Athenian fleet of seventy-six ships, under the command of Thrasyllus and Thrasybulus, was beached off the town of Elæus, just inside the entrance to the Hellespont on the European shore. The allied fleet of eighty-eight ships, under the command of Mindarus, lay off Abydus, some fifteen sea miles up the Hellespont on the Asiatic shore. Both fleets had been in those positions for five whole days. On the sixth day the Athenians advanced up the Hellespont in single line ahead, keeping along the European shore. Thrasyllus commanded the van or left wing, Thrasybulus the rear or right wing. On the Athenian movement being reported the allied fleet left Abydus and moved down the Hellespont, also in single line ahead along the Asiatic shore. Thucydides states that the allies' line stretched from Abydus to Dardanus, a distance of about six and a half sea miles, which represents an average interval of about 150 yards, or about three ships' lengths from stem to stem. On the same basis the length of the Athenian line would have been about five and three-quarter sea miles. No doubt the intervals between the ships were closer in some parts of each line—perhaps only two ships' lengths, or 100 yards from stem to stem—and wider in others, as in the case of the Athenian centre, which

---

[1] Thu., viii. 104, 105.

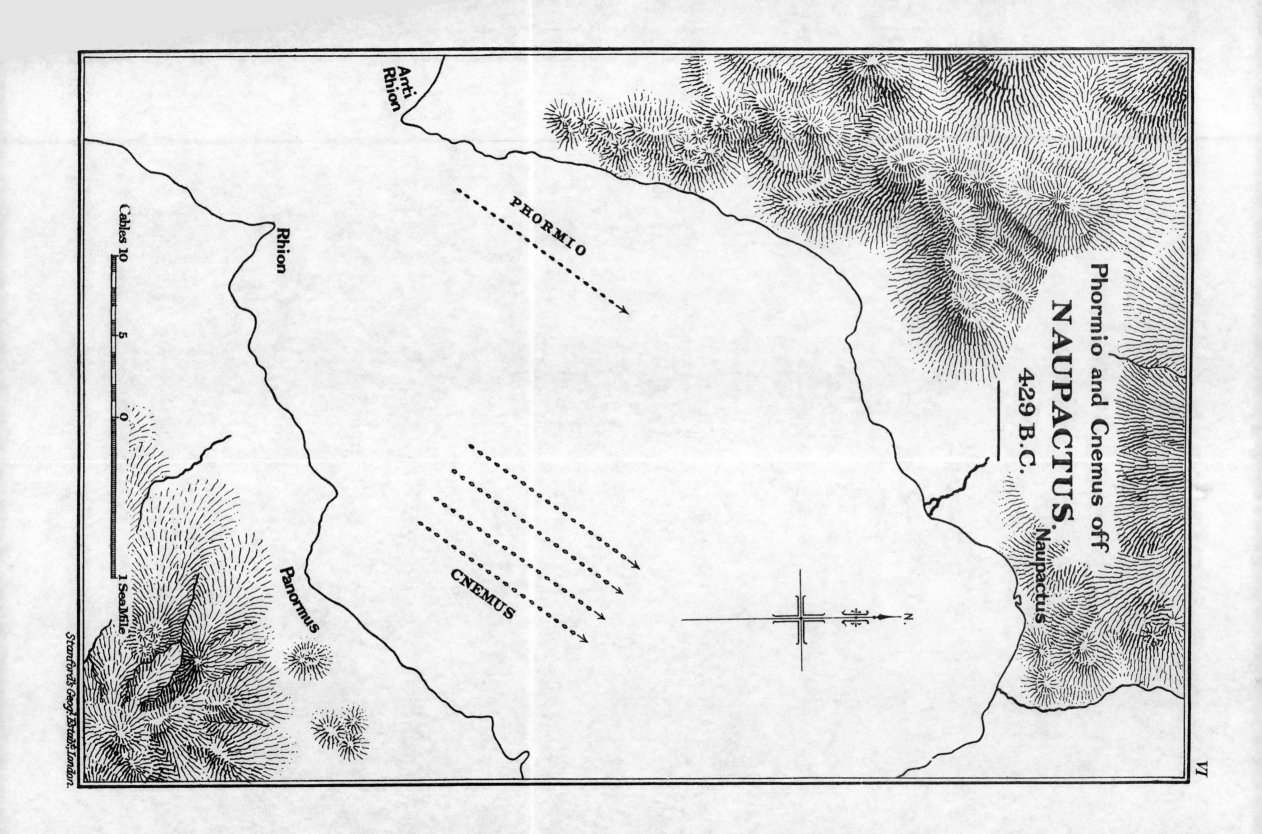

Phormio and Cnemus off
NAUPACTUS.
429 B.C.

PHORMIO

CNEMUS

Naupactus

Arti
Rhion

Rhion

Panormus

Cables 10   5   0   1 Sea Mile

Stanford's Geog.¹ Estab.ᵗ London.

N.

VI

Thucydides speaks of as being "thinned and weakened." Moreover, the tendency to straggle in the Athenian line was probably greater than in the allied, because the former had rowed against the current three times as far as the latter with it.

When the two centres were in the Narrows, and the allied van or left wing was either abreast, or nearly abreast, of Dardanus, and either overlapping, or about to overlap, the Athenian rear or right wing, Thrasybulus turned his division and rowed down the Hellespont to prevent the overlap. He succeeded in doing so, and thus prevented his flank being doubled on by Mindarus, whose division was superior in numbers.

While Mindarus and Thrasybulus were rowing hard down the Hellespont, the remainder of the two fleets came into action. The allied centre attacked and defeated the Athenian centre; the numbers here were nearly equal, but the Athenian ships had straggled, and the distance between the two lines in or near the Narrows cannot have been more than 1000 yards, which left them at a disadvantage and much exposed to attack by ships in closer order. On seeing the confusion in the centre, resulting from the defeat and pursuit, Thrasybulus turned his division, thus stopping further extension, attacked and defeated Mindarus. The particular form given to this attack has not come down to us.[1] He then fell on the scattered allied ships in the centre and put them to flight.

Meanwhile Thrasyllus, on the other wing, had been engaged and fully occupied with the Syracusans and other ships equal in numbers to his own. At last they also gave way when they saw the allied ships in the centre flying. The Athenians captured twenty-one ships and lost fifteen. Their victory was not very pronounced, seeing that while the Athenians advanced into the Propontis and captured the eight allied ships in Byzantine waters, the allies moved down to Elæus and recovered some of their captured ships.

We are to note that neither side seems to have possessed any marked superiority either in the speed of the ships, or in their numbers, or in their individual fighting power, and

---

[1] Cf. The action between Cnemus and Phormio off Naupactus in 429.

therefore that neither side attempted to force a battle in the open sea or to make use of the land. The selection of the battle-site was not influenced by tactical conditions, as at Salamis; on the contrary, the tactics conformed to the requirements of the site. The numbers being nearly equal, the reciprocal aim was to bring as large a force as possible into action. Hence the two fleets deployed along the opposite shores of the Hellespont, and in single line, because the waters were narrow. The allied attempts to use their numerical superiority to outflank was met by moving the whole Athenian right wing to the flank.[1] Since the numbers on either side in the centre were nearly equal, the Athenian failure there was probably due not so much to the withdrawal of the right wing as to their ships not being well closed up. The battle illustrates a step in the development of tactics, in that the centre and one wing were held by a frontal attack while an attempt was made to outflank the other wing.

CALLICRATIDAS AND THRASYBULUS (?) OFF ARGINUSÆ, AUGUST 406 B.C.

The last battle at sea, during the war, possessing any tactical interest, was fought off the Arginusæ Islands, seemingly in August 406 (Plan VIII.). The facts, as far as known, are that Callicratidas with one hundred and twenty allied ships, of which most had been manned for a long time, was at Malea, the south-eastern point of Lesbos. The Athenian fleet of one hundred and fifty ships, all hastily manned only two months earlier, was at the Arginusæ Islands, eight sea miles to the east. The name of the Athenian admiral is not known for certain, but Thrasybulus has been mentioned as commanding on the day of the battle.[2] Six miles north of Malea was Eteonicus with fifty allied ships watching Conon with forty Athenians at Mitylene. These ships took no part in the battle. At daybreak Callicratidas put to sea and steered for the Arginusæ Islands, off which the Athenians met his attack.

On contact the allied fleet was ranged in a single line

---

[1] Cf. Lepanto, 1571 A.D.   [2] Diodorus, xiii. c. 14.

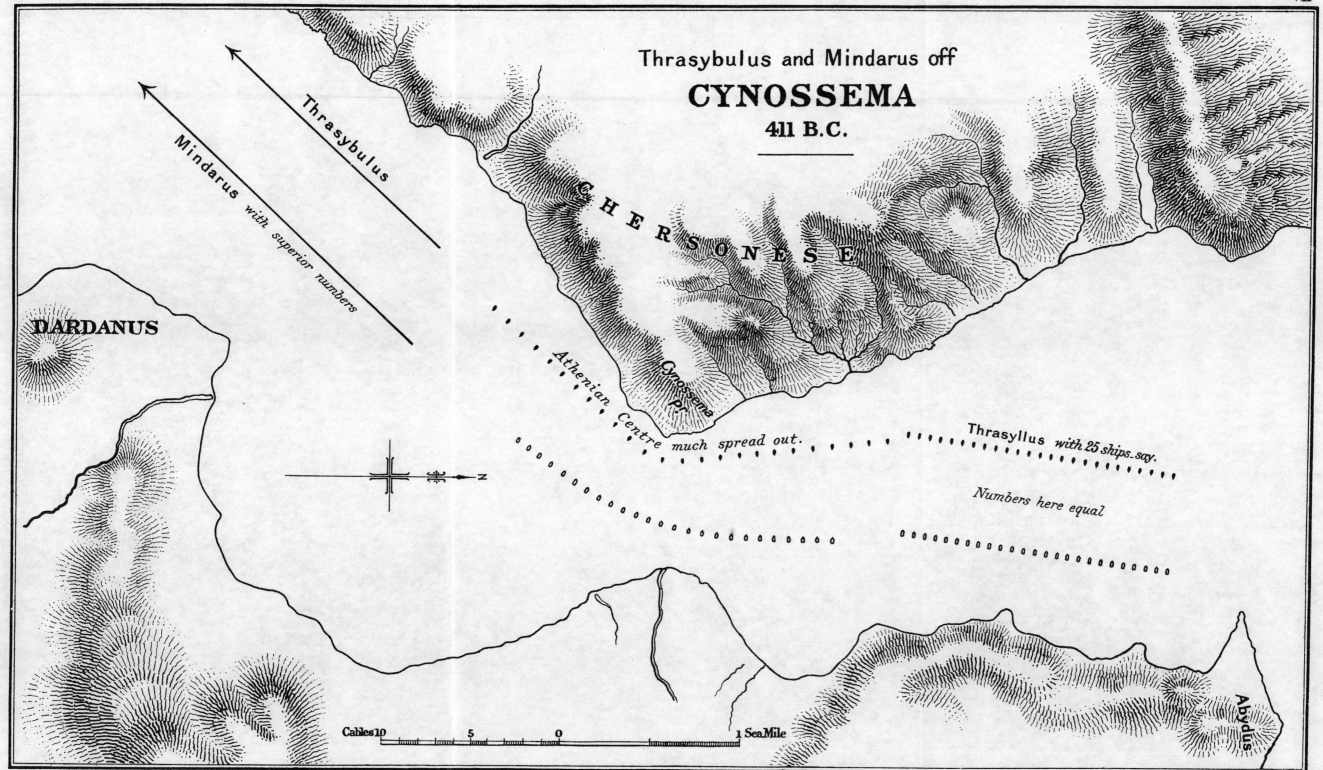

VII

Thrasybulus and Mindarus off

CYNOSSEMA
411 B.C.

Thrasybulus

Mindarus with superior numbers

DARDANUS

C H E R S O N E S E

Cynossema pr

Athenian Centre much spread out.

Thrasyllus with 25 ships say.

Numbers here equal

N

Abydus

Cables 10   5   0   1 Sea Mile

Stanford's Geog.¹ Estab.ᵗ London.

Thrasybulus and Mindarus of
CYNOSSEMA
411 B.C.

abreast, which, as the ships cannot have been less than two ships' lengths—100 yards—apart, extended certainly not less than six and probably seven sea miles. Nothing is known of its organisation, except that Callicratidas commanded the right wing, including the Lacedæmonian contingent of ten ships, and Thrasonidas, a Theban, the left wing where the Bœotian and Eubœan ships were stationed. The Athenian fleet was formed in two lines abreast, the one disposed astern of the other—an arrangement which probably gave good opportunities to the ships in the second line when those in the first line were in collision or otherwise entangled with the enemy. Each wing consisted of four divisions, two in the front line and two in the rear; each division numbered fifteen ships. The centre was more lightly held by a front line of twenty ships, possibly opened out slightly, and was supported by ten ships in the second line. The Athenian front must have covered four to five sea miles, or even more. The allied overlap was nearly two miles, which means that upwards of thirty of their ships delivered their charge "in the air" and were for a certain time not in the fight. That interval was probably not short, since ordinary men under such circumstances usually wait for orders.[1]

The Athenian dispositions seem designed to hold the centre with a force equal to that of the enemy, while two masses, each of sixty ships, were launched against the thirty ships on either side of the centre; in other words, their aim was to throw their whole fleet of one hundred and fifty ships on to eighty or ninety of the enemy with the view of getting a decision before the ships in the overlap could come into action. The result was a complete defeat of the allies, who lost seventy-seven triremes as against twenty-five lost by the Athenians.

If the above view is correct, the tactical skill of the Athenians in the battle was of a high order. The conditions were novel. The fleets approached each other over an open sea, and their movements were not circumscribed as at Cynossema in the narrow waters of the Hellespont. The numbers engaged were much larger than those at Corcyra

---

[1] Cf. Franco-Spanish van at Trafalgar in 1805; also French ships to leeward at the Nile in 1798.

and Naupactus, and neither side probably possessed any marked superiority in speed. Hence Phormio's tactics were no longer applicable. The Athenians used their superior numbers to strike not at the wings to envelope, but at the centre to break through, which they seem to have done, seeing that the fleets " at first fought in a close body and afterwards separately."

According to Xenophon, the Athenians were drawn up in two lines to prevent their own line being broken through; for their ships were slower and less handy than those of the enemy. The Lacedæmonians were arranged in single line with a view to breaking through the enemy and then turning to ram; for their ships were faster and handier. He dwells on skill in handling a single ship—*i.e.*, in ramming, rather than on that in bringing a fleet into battle. He emphasises the advantage of the double line in defence, but omits all reference to the strength of the Athenian dispositions in attack.[1] He seems not to have realised the significance of his own words, which is not surprising if he had no practical knowledge of the management of fleets, as is probable. Moreover, it is not unusual for contemporaries, including uninstructed professional men, to misunderstand and misrepresent battles at sea—*e.g.*, Trafalgar and other instances.

[1] Xen., *Hell.*, i. ch. 6.

VIII

CALLICRATIDAS AND THRASYBULUS(?)

at Arginusae – August 406.

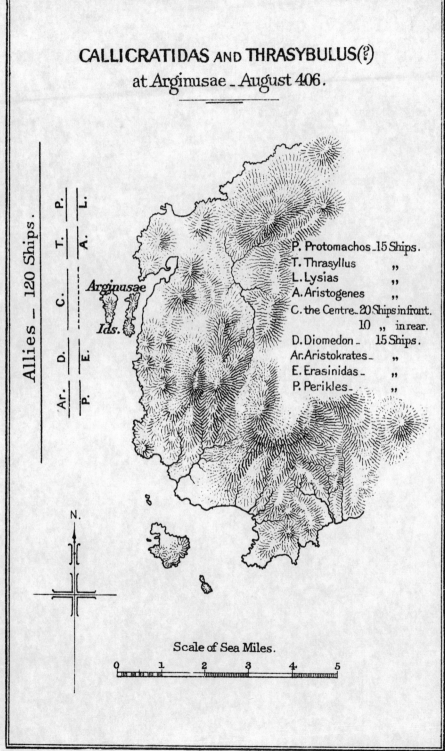

Allies – 120 Ships.

P.   T.   P.
    L.
C.   A.

Ar.   D.
    E.   P.

Arginusae
Ids.

P. Protomachos _ 15 Ships.
T. Thrasyllus   ,,
L. Lysias   ,,
A. Aristogenes   ,,
C. the Centre _ 20 Ships in front.
            10   ,,   in rear.
D. Diomedon _   15 Ships.
Ar. Aristokrates _   ,,
E. Erasinidas _   ,,
P. Perikles _   ,,

N.

Scale of Sea Miles.

0   1   2   3   4   5

Stanford's Geog.ª Estabᵗ London.

VII.

THE OPERATIONS.

THE TEN YEARS' WAR.

AT the outbreak of the Peloponnesian War, the Greek world was split into two great divisions:—
1. The Athenian empire with its allies.
2. The Lacedæmonian league, or the Peloponnesians as often spoken of.

The Athenian empire consisted of Athens—the leading, governing, and dominant state—and a number of other city states which, with two exceptions, Chios and Lesbos, paid tribute to her. These tributary city states were to be found on the coasts of Caria, Ionia, the Hellespont, and Thrace, and included all the islands east of the line from the Peloponnesus to Crete, except Melos and Thera. Although originally a voluntary league, it had become a maritime empire held together by force, as was shown by the treatment of the tributary city states—*e.g.*, Naxos[1] and Mitylene,[2] which were both reduced by force after revolting. Moreover, if Thucydides is correct, Athens pressed the right of the stronger to rule the weaker both in their reply to the Corinthians at Lacedæmon before the war,[3] and in the Melian controversy after the peace of Nicias.[4] The allies of Athens included in western Greece, the Acarnanians, the Messenians of Naupactus, Corcyra (Corfu) and Zacynthus (Zante); in central and northern Greece, Platæa and Thessaly.[5]

The Lacedæmonian league was headed by Sparta, and included states which were not tributaries, but were governed

---

[1] Thu., i. 98.   [2] Ibid., iii. 35, 36.   [3] Ibid., i. 76.
[4] Ibid., v. 85-112.   [5] Ibid., ii. 9, 22.

by oligarchies in her interest.[1] These allied states included the whole Peloponnesus, except Argos and Achaia; Corinth and Megara on or near the Isthmus; Ambracia, Anactorium, and Leucas in western Greece; Bœotia, Phocis, and Locris in northern Greece.[2] It was a league of states on the mainland, brought together chiefly by fear of the Athenian sea power, strengthened by the antagonism between the two rival systems of government then dividing the Greek world —the democratic and the oligarchic—and further stiffened by the commercial rivalry between Athens and Corinth.

The political object of the war was on the one side extension of the rule of force, and on the other security against any such extension. This meant a collision between the armed forces. Hence the reciprocal military aim was primarily to destroy or to neutralise the action of the armed forces, and secondarily to impair the resources on which the armed forces depended.

The actual strength of the armed forces on either side is not exactly known. The Athenian Navy was said at the outbreak of the war to number more than two hundred and fifty triremes;[3] Corcyra furnished fifty ships on one occasion,[4] Chios and Lesbos jointly the same number on another.[5] The Peloponnesian Navy was drawn chiefly from Corinth, Megara, Sicyon, Pellene inside the Gulf, and from Elis, Ambracia, and Leucas[6] outside, but the number of ships is not known. Nevertheless it is certain that the Athenian Navy was much the stronger of the two. On the land the case was different, since the Athenian army was far outnumbered.[7] It is to be remembered that on each side the armed force was liable to be diverted from taking action against the enemy to overawing or to quelling revolt among the disaffected, as, for instance, the tribute-paying city states of Athens, and the helot or servile population of Sparta.

The principal armed force was to be found at sea on the one side, and on land on the other side; thus, the two could not come into full and direct collision. The weaker army, when challenged, refused battle and withdrew behind the impregnable walls of Athens, where in free communication

---

[1] Thu., i. 19.   [2] Ibid., ii. 9.   [3] Ibid., iii. 17.   [4] Ibid., ii. 25.
[5] Ibid., ii. 56.   [6] Ibid., ii. 9.   [7] Ibid., i. 143.

with the sea it drew supplies from the outside world.[1] No
direct and systematic action was taken against the weaker
Peloponnesian Navy. Hence the outstanding feature of the
operations was that the primary military aim fell into the
background, and the secondary military aims were free to
come to the front on each side.

The resources on which the armed forces depended were
man power and food; wealth, manufactures, and natural
products which were exchanged for food, and shipping which
effected that exchange.

Of the man power or populations engaged in the war, no
sufficiently accurate information is available, but it is to be
noted that the larger part on both sides was in a state of
slavery, and therefore a source of weakness.

The home-grown food supply of ancient as of modern
Greece was quite insufficient for the wants of the inhabitants,
and was largely supplemented by corn imported from the
Euxine, Egypt, and Sicily.[2]

In wealth, as Pericles is said to have remarked, Athens
possessed an advantage in that she had accumulated before
the outbreak of the war a treasure of about £1,500,000, and
derived from her tributary states an income of about £120,000
per annum.[3] The Peloponnesians had no such resources.

The manufacturing states were Athens on the one side,
and Corinth, Megara, and Sicyon on the other side. The
natural products on which the remaining states chiefly
depended were derived from the vine and the olive.

The carrying trade was in the hands of Athens on the one
side, and of Corinth on the other; the former controlling
more especially the trade to the Euxine, and the latter that
to the west of the Gulf of Corinth.

Of these resources the most important was food. At the
outset the operations were mainly directed against the home
supply, under the belief that the enemy would be obliged to
fight or to come to terms if his growing crops were threatened.
Up to that time this had been the accepted Greek theory of
war. During the first seven years—431 to 425—the hostile
armies cross-raided Attica and the Megarid respectively,

---

[1] Cf. Wellington at Torres Vedras, 1810.
[2] Thu., iii. 86 ; vii. 28 ; iv. 53.   [3] Ibid., ii. 13.

ravaging the country from which the inhabitants had previously been withdrawn inside the walled towns, at that time impregnable.   No serious attempt was made on either side to resist these raids, which were of short duration owing to difficulties of supply and other causes.   Moreover, the sufferings of the Megarid were not felt in the Peloponnesus, and the inhabitants of Attica were not solely dependent on the growing crops, since supplies from oversea were secured by the long walls connecting Athens with the Piræus, built nearly thirty years earlier.   The popular pressure to take he offensive on land was at times strong in Athens, but Pericles, the great Athenian leader, was able to resist any such action.   Thus no battle on land resulted, but such was the popular emotion caused by the destruction of the countryside, by the suffering due to overcrowding, and to a serious outbreak of plague, that in the second year of the war (430) Athens made overtures for peace, which met with no success. The hitherto accepted theory of war had failed.[1]   Neither a decision by battle nor a peace by agreement had resulted. In order to oblige Athens to fight or to come to terms, it was necessary to threaten the imported as well as the home-grown food supply, but this may not have been generally appreciated, although suggested by Archidamus the Spartan king before the outbreak of the war.[2]

Similarly, the Athenian fleet raided nearly every year the coast districts of the Peloponnesus, and with even less effect. Gradually seems to have come a glimmer that the true rôle of the stronger navy was to operate against the imported rather than the home-grown food—to stop the enemy's trade.   The trade route mainly disputed was that to Sicily, which ran out of the Gulf of Corinth up the coast to Corcyra, thence across to and down the coast of Italy.   This was the regular route for rowing ships of war, since it involved the shortest passage from land to land—about sixty miles—as against upwards of two hundred miles of open sea by the direct route, which may perhaps have been followed by some merchant ships.   At that time these were dependent on sails, and used oars only as an auxiliary.

During the first year of the war the Athenian fleet captured

[1] Thu., ii. 59-65.   [2] Ibid., i. 81.

the Corinthian settlements at Sollium and Astacus on the coast of Acarnania and won over the island of Cephallenia,[1] which, with Corcyra and Zacynthus, already their allies, strengthened their hold on this route. But as the fleet returned home, leaving no naval force in those waters, that hold was insecure. The Peloponnesian fleet was able to raid both Cephallenia and Zacynthus and to recapture Astacus.[2] Moreover, trade at sea cannot be stopped by simply occupying islands. It is evident that Athens required in those waters the continual presence of a naval force to neutralise the activities of the Peloponnesian fleet. This need may have been recognised, since in the second winter of the war (430) Phormio, with twenty triremes, was sent to Naupactus,[3] where he not only interposed between the enemies' squadrons inside and outside the Gulf, but was in a favourable position to stop their trade. To reopen the trade route became a necessity for Corinth and the Peloponnesus. The plan proposed by the Ambraciots, and accepted by the Peloponnesians, was a combined attack to overrun Acarnania, after which Naupactus might be captured, also Cephallenia and Zacynthus might fall into their hands.[4] The land power proposed to seize the naval bases, without which the Athenian fleet would be unable to obtain supplies of food, and would be without the indispensable landing-places on which to beach their ships and to disembark their crews. Corcyra, one hundred miles to the north, being too distant to use as a base, the success of the plan would mean the withdrawal of the Athenian fleet and the opening of the trade route. Its execution was intrusted to Cnemus the Spartan, who with a few ships and a thousand Lacedæmonian hoplites evaded Phormio and crossed from the Peloponnesus to Leucas, where the ships from cities outside the Gulf also assembled. Cnemus collected a land force from the Corinthian settlements in that region and from the tribes of the interior; he then advanced without waiting for the co-operation of the contingents from Corinth and other places inside the Gulf. The details of the land operations do not concern us. It will suffice to say that he was defeated and forced to retreat to

---

[1] Thu., ii. 30.   [2] Ibid., ii. 33.
[3] Ibid., ii. 69.   [4] Ibid., ii. 80.

Œniadæ, near the mouth of the river Achelous.[1] Meanwhile Phormio defeated Machaôn and dispersed the squadron
bringing reinforcements from Corinth and other cities, as
has been already related.[2] The defeated ships withdrew to
Cyllene, the Peloponnesian dockyard and naval base in Elis,
where they were joined by Cnemus and the ships from
Leucas.[3] The expedition had completely failed. It seems
to have been now realised that the proposed plan could not
be carried out until Phormio's ships had been destroyed or
their action otherwise neutralised. Cnemus was told that he
must fight again. Moreover, three Lacedæmonian commissioners, one of whom was the celebrated Brasidas, were sent
to advise him. On their arrival they and Cnemus called on
the allied cities to furnish additional ships, and pressed on
the refit of those at Cyllene.

Phormio, on his part, warned the Athenians of the impending battle, and asked for large and immediate reinforcements. They sent him twenty ships, but evidently without
understanding the importance of his work or the urgency
of his need. Unlike Themistocles, they did not realise that
the primary aim of the fleet should be to destroy the enemy's
armed ships, nor did they recognise the value of time. The
commander of the reinforcement was ordered to call on his
way at Crete and to take part in a petty local quarrel between
two Cretan towns.[4] The delay due to this service, as also to
contrary winds and bad weather, was such that the reinforcements arrived too late for the battle, in which Phormio suffered
such heavy losses and was so nearly defeated, as has been
already related. It is evident that his victories were due to
his own courage and leading, backed by the skill and valour
of his officers and men, rather than to the dispositions
arranged in Athens. The effect of those victories was that
the plan to seize the Athenian naval bases in the west was
defeated.

The presence of Athenian detachments in any strength
seems from now onwards to have been intermittent in western
waters. They were used mainly in connection with land
operations to consolidate the Athenian hold on Acarnania,
and thus ultimately to insure the safety of the naval bases

---

[1] Thu., ii. 81, 82.　　[2] P. 35 *supra*.　　[3] Thu., ii. 84.　　[4] Ibid., ii. 85.

in that region rather than against the enemy's ships. For example, Phormio, after leading an expedition into Acarnania in the winter of 429, returned with his ships to Athens in the following spring.[1] Again, in the summer of 428 his place at Naupactus was taken by his son Asopius, who made an abortive attempt on Œniadæ and later effected a landing in Leucas, where he was defeated and slain.[2] Furthermore, two summers later (426) the enterprising Demosthenes, the son of Alcisthenes, with thirty Athenian triremes, was sent there.[3] Assisted by contingents from the allies of Athens in that region, including Corcyra, he over-ran Leucadian territory. Instead of completing his work there by blockading and reducing the walled city of Leucas, which would have permanently strengthened the Athenian hold on that region and on the western trade route, he initiated an expedition into Ætolia with the object of passing through that country into Phocis and thence into Bœotia. This ill-considered plan, which started with an attempt to force a passage through a mountainous country inhabited by warlike and hostile tribes, alienated some of his allies, and resulted not only in his complete defeat but in the withdrawal of the remnant of his force to Athens and of himself to Naupactus.[4] Moreover, on the call for help from Ætolia, the Peloponnesians in the autumn launched a counterstroke by land from Delphi against that naval base, which was held successfully by Demosthenes with help from Acarnania. Eurylochus, the Lacedæmonian commander, having failed to take Naupactus, now dismissed his Ætolian allies, but remained in the country.[5] In the winter he advanced north to co-operate with the Ambraciots on the shores of the Ambracian Gulf, where he and his allies were totally defeated with heavy losses by Demosthenes at the head of the local forces, aided by an Athenian squadron of twenty ships which entered that Gulf. These defeats put an end to the war on land in that region, and made Naupactus safe,[6] but the Athenian hold on the islands and on the western trade route remained insecure so long as the Peloponnesian fleet was not put out of action.

---

[1] Thu., ii. 102, 103.   [2] Ibid., iii. 7.   [3] Ibid., iii. 91.
[4] Ibid., iii. 94-97.   [5] Ibid., iii. 101, 102.   [6] Ibid., 105-114.

It is now necessary to turn to the second great resource on which Athens relied—viz., the wealth in the shape of tribute at her disposal. One of the original causes of the war was the siege of Potidæa, a town in Chalcidicé, originally a colony of Corinth, but then an Athenian tributary state, which with other cities had revolted at the instigation of Macedonia in the year 432, and had received aid from Corinth.[1] Athens sent a fleet and army to put down the revolt and to blockade Potidæa, which did not surrender until 430.[2] It is not necessary to dwell upon the operations in Chalcidicé, which did not cease until the following year, as they are of no particular interest except as an example of the drain on the fleet, army, and wealth of Athens, caused by operations excentric to the main effort against the Peloponnesus.

Furthermore, the war, especially at sea, was influenced by the revolt of Mitylene and other cities in the island of Lesbos during the year 428.[3] These cities did not pay tribute, but were bound by the terms of their alliance with Athens to furnish contingents of ships. The danger of the revolt in Lesbos as in Chalcidicé was that if either Mitylene or Potidæa were permitted to withdraw from the alliance, other cities might follow their example, and Athens might thus lose the tribute upon which the maintenance of her navy largely depended. That this was a real and widespread danger is further borne out by the attack on and defeat of Lysicles when collecting tribute about this time in Caria, where he had been sent with a squadron of twelve ships.[4]

The first news of the disaffection in Lesbos reached Athens early in the year, but it was not until the spring—say in May, when the annual Peloponnesian raid into Attica took place—that Cleïppides with forty ships was diverted from the usual raid on the coast of the Peloponnesus to reduce Mitylene to submission.[5] The operations were protracted, and are of no special interest. In the autumn—say October—reinforcements arrived under the command of Paches.[6] The city was then completely blockaded by land and sea, and surrendered in the following spring—say May 427.[7] Thus, as in Chalcidicé,

---

[1] Thu., i. 58-60.   [2] Ibid., i. 61 *et seq.*; ii. 70.   [3] Ibid., iii. 2.
[4] Ibid., iii. 19.   [5] Ibid., iii. 3.   [6] Ibid., iii. 18.   [7] Ibid., iii. 28.

a considerable force was employed for a whole year not against the principal enemy—the Peloponnesians—but in making good the weakness inherent in the Athenian empire owing to its too exclusive dependence on force.

But this was not the only effect on the general operations produced by the Lesbos revolt. On the first appearance of the Athenian fleet Mitylene appealed to, and in July 428 entered into alliance with, Lacedæmon, who agreed to make a diversion by a joint attack on Attica by land and sea, the ships being provided by transporting them across the Isthmus of Corinth from the Gulf. Although the orders to mobilise were at once issued by Lacedæmon, that promise was not fulfilled, partly because her allies found it difficult to assemble their armies during the summer—say in August—when the crops were being gathered, and partly because the Athenians provided an unexpected counterstroke in the shape of a fleet of one hundred triremes, with which, after parading their strength along the shores of the Isthmus, they made descents on the Peloponnesus,[1] as also did Asopius with a detached squadron of thirty ships. Finally, neither side having achieved any real result, both returned home, except Asopius, who, as already mentioned, proceeded with twelve ships to Naupactus.[2]

The diversion against Attica having failed to weaken the Athenian effort against Mitylene, the Peloponnesians now ordered a fleet of forty-two ships to be equipped for its relief. That fleet was not ready and did not put to sea until the following year (427), shortly before the annual raid into Attica—say the end of April.[3] The relieving force was wanting in the condition essential to success. It was no more than about equal in numbers to the blockading fleet, and therefore, on the relative efficiency shown in every action during the early years of the war, not strong enough to fight and defeat that force. That Alcidas the Lacedæmonian admiral was of that opinion, is manifest from his action throughout. He displayed no ardent desire to fight,—the sure sign of a leader uncertain of himself and of the strength of his force; he lost time about the Peloponnesus, and proceeded so leisurely—probably *via* Melos—that on arrival

---

[1] Thu., iii. 15, 16.   [2] P. 51 *supra*.   [3] Thu., iii. 26.

E

at Myconus or Icaria he found that Mitylene had fallen.
To obtain confirmation of the news he proceeded to Embatum,
a port—position uncertain—on the coast of Erythræ, some
fifty to sixty sea miles south of Mitylene, where he learnt
that the surrender had taken place seven days before—say
in May.[1]

It is proper to note that his delay may in part have been
due to difficulties in thej supply of food for his crews of
perhaps nine thousand men, as to which Thucydides is silent.
As the stowage of his ships was very limited, he must have
depended either on victuallers, which could not have had the
speed of his triremes, or on the local resources at the ports
of call, where food may not have been easily collected.   In
either case delay may have been caused.

Be that as it may, Alcidas had now to settle his future
movements. He received a proposal to surprise and recapture
Mitylene, which was inadmissible so long as the Athenian
fleet was present and undefeated. He rejected that proposal,
as also a suggestion to occupy a town in Ionia, where, as
was admitted, he would be blockaded, but might, nevertheless, be able to raise the standard of revolt throughout the
country. No one seems to have suggested a battle with
the Athenian fleet; Alcidas least of all, if Thucydides is
correct in saying that his sole idea was to get back as fast
as he could to the Peloponnesus.[2] That seems to have been
the case, as he sailed from Embatum and proceeded south
along the coast to Ephesus, being sighted *en route* and
reported by two detached Athenian triremes.[3] Paches, while
occupied with operations at Lesbos, consequent on the fall
of Mitylene, had received the unexpected news that a
Peloponnesian fleet had arrived on the coast of Erythræ.
He was eager for battle, and at once started in pursuit.
From Ephesus Alcidas fled to Crete, chased as far as Patmos
by Paches, who, having failed to overtake the enemy, returned
to Lesbos, calling *en route* at Notium.[4] Paches' proceedings
at either place, as also the tragic escape of the inhabitants
of Mitylene, do not concern us.

Alcidas' ships were dispersed by a gale of wind on the
passage to Crete, and subsequently straggled back to Cyllene,

[1] Thu., iii. 29.　　[2] Ibid., iii. 30, 31.　　[3] Ibid., iii. 33.　　[4] Ibid., iii. 33, 34.

probably during the month of June.[1] He had captured a few merchant ships during the cruise, and had massacred most of their crews after leaving Embatum. Beyond that the expedition had achieved no results, probably because the admiral had either insufficient means, or insufficient will, to carry out the service intrusted to him. It seems possible either that the Peloponnesians did not realise the relative inefficiency of their fleet, or that they did not understand that the relief of Mitylene depended upon putting the Athenian fleet out of action.

But the revolt of Lesbos was not the only indirect attempt to weaken Athens. While she was occupied at Mitylene in the year 427, civil war between the oligarchy and democracy broke out in Corcyra at the instigation of Corinth. This was brought about through the medium of well-to-do prisoners—members of the oligarchic party—who had been captured at the battle of Sybota in the year 433-2. These men, after being won over, were released and sent home with the understanding that they were, if possible, to detach Corcyra from the Athenian alliance. The details of the civil war do not concern us.[2] It is sufficient to say that when the disturbances began in the summer, Nicostratus with twelve Athenian triremes proceeded to Corcyra from Naupactus. His arrival strengthened the democratic party, who had already gained the upper hand. He was about to leave for Naupactus, when Alcidas with fifty-three triremes and Brasidas as his adviser arrived from Cyllene and anchored off Sybota.[3] On the morrow occurred the action at sea already described.[4] The victory of Alcidas might have given temporary control to the oligarchy, if he had at once occupied the town. Instead of doing that the next day was wasted in landing and ravaging the south part of the island.[5] He thus missed his opportunity, since at nightfall came from Leucas, some fifty miles distant, a signal announcing the approach of sixty Athenian triremes, which had been specially sent from Athens under Eurymedon.[6] The very same night Alcidas sailed on his return home. He evaded the advancing Eurymedon by keeping close under the land and by hauling his

[1] Thu., iii. 69. [2] Ibid., iii. 70. [3] Ibid., iii. 75, 76.
[4] P. 36 *supra*. [5] Thu., iii. 79. [6] Ibid., iii. 80.

ships across the Leucadian Isthmus.[1] The arrival of the
Athenian fleet secured the control of the democratic party
and the alliance between Corcyra and Athens, but it was not
until two years later, after the surrender of the Peloponnesian
fleet at Pylus, that the armed resistance of the oligarchic
party was finally suppressed.[2] The reader will note that
possibly the raid of Alcidas on the coast of Ionia might have
been prevented, the resistance of Mitylene shortened, and a
deterrent provided against civil war in Corcyra, if instead of
making comparatively futile short raids at long intervals on
the coast of the Peloponnesus, a strong detachment of the
Athenian fleet had been kept in position to bring to action
any Peloponnesian ships which put to sea from Cyllene or
issued from the Gulf. The reasons for not doing so are
doubtful, but may have been either difficulties of manning and
supply, or failure to understand that the destruction of the
armed force was as necessary at sea as it was then admitted
to be on land. However that may have been, the Athenian
hold on the trade route to Sicily had not been permanently
reduced, as it would have been if Corcyra and her large fleet
had passed over to the side of the Peloponnesians.

To strengthen her control of the trade in the west, Athens
now sent at the end of the same summer (427) a squadron of
twenty ships to Sicily in response to an appeal from Leontini
and other cities for help in their war with Syracuse and her
allies. According to Thucydides the real Athenian aim was
to check at the source the export of corn from Sicily to the
Peloponnesus, and included even the possible control of
affairs in the island.[3] A naval force was maintained there
until the year 424, when the Sicilian cities concluded a peace
among themselves and the Athenians withdrew.[4] The operations in Sicilian waters were secondary and largely excentric
to the main issue, diverted a considerable force from the
attack on the principal enemy, and were in their larger aim
opposed to the warning originally given by Pericles not to
attempt any extension of the Athenian empire during the
war.[5] During the year 426, in addition to the operations in
Sicily and Acarnania already mentioned,[6] Athens sent a large

---

[1] Thu., iii. 81.   [2] P. 60 *infra.*   [3] Thu., iii. 86,
[4] Ibid., iv. 65.   [5] Ibid., i. 144.   [6] Pp. 51 *supra.*

force of sixty triremes and 2000 hoplites, under the command of Nicias, to ravage the island of Melos. This force then proceeded to Oropus, and in conjunction with a land force from Athens ravaged the territory of Tanagra. The fleet afterwards raided Locris.[1] This expedition not being directed against the principal enemy, was largely a waste of force.

We have now reached the year 425, the seventh of the war, which saw a great change in its conduct, due partly to the influence of Demosthenes, who had returned to Athens with the prestige arising from his victories in Acarnania, and partly to the unforeseen march of events. The essential facts are that in the spring Demosthenes embarked on board a fleet of forty triremes bound to Sicily under the command of Eurymedon and another officer. On the one hand, Eurymedon had orders to call at Corcyra, and to assist the democrats in the city against the oligarchs, who had established themselves in the mountains and were ravaging the island. On the other hand, Demosthenes seems to have been authorised to use the fleet on the coast of the Peloponnesus according to his judgment. On reaching the west coast, the former wanted to advance and to bring to action the Peloponnesian fleet of sixty ships, then reported to be either at Corcyra or bound thither; the latter wished to put in at the Bay of Pylus (Navarin). Stress of weather solved the difficulty and drove the fleet to take shelter in that harbour, where, at the instigation of Demosthenes in the face of strong opposition, the Pylus peninsula was seized and fortified. Leaving five ships with that officer to hold the fort, Eurymedon proceeded with the remainder for Corcyra.[2] As soon as the occupation became known at Sparta, the Peloponnesian army, then raiding Attica, was withdrawn, a land force was sent to Pylus, and the Peloponnesian fleet was ordered from Corcyra to the same place. This fleet slipped unobserved past the Athenians while at Zacynthus on their way north, but before its arrival Demosthenes sent two of his ships to warn Eurymedon of the impending attack and to ask for aid.[3]

The Bay of Pylus (Plan IX.) is a large sheet of water, nearly three sea miles long by two broad, enclosed between the mainland and the island of Sphacteria, which bounds it on the

[1] Thu., iii. 91. [2] Ibid., iv. 2-5. [3] Ibid., iv. 6-8.

west, and is about 4800 yards long. North of the Bay and
separated from it by a sand-bar is a lagoon. The Pylus
peninsula, held by the Athenians, lies at the north-west corner
of the Bay, and is now connected with the mainland by the
isthmus which separates Voithio Kilia from the lagoon, and
by the aforesaid sand-bar. In the year 425 the isthmus
seems to have been in existence, but the sand-bar may either
have not yet formed or have been cut off by a channel
running close under Pylus, and connecting the Bay with
the lagoon which may have been navigable and used
as a harbour. There are two entrances to the Bay—the
southern, twelve hundred yards wide,[1] which, as Thucydides
very reasonably says, was wide enough to admit eight or
nine triremes in line abreast;[2] the northern, dividing
Sphacteria from Pylus, less than two hundred yards wide,
now silted up, but which would then admit two triremes
abreast, since two columns in line ahead could be closed to
less than two ships' lengths, whereas a line abreast could not
without sacrificing power of manœuvring. Both Sphacteria
and Pylus were at that time strong defensible positions.
Demosthenes beached his three ships, protected them with
a stockade, and made the best arrangements for defence
possible. For his rowers weapons were obtained from two
Messenian privateers which happened to be in the harbour,
but some men remained unarmed. The Peloponnesians on
their arrival occupied Sphacteria and the practicable shores
of the Bay on the mainland, thus narrowly restricting for
the Athenians the possibility of landing—an indispensable
necessity for the crews of a fleet in those days. They then
prepared to storm the Pylus position. When their preparations were complete, the army assaulted on the north-east
land side; the fleet of forty-three ships, working in relays,
owing to the narrow beach available, endeavoured to disembark its men on the south-west sea front. After re-
peated attempts, prolonged over a day and a half, the attack
failed.[3]

---

[1] Admiralty Chart, No. 211.

[2] The topography is discussed in the ' Journal of Hellenic Studies,' vol. xvi.   G. B.
Grundy.

[3] Thu., iv, 9-13.

Presently Eurymedon returned with his fleet reinforced to fifty ships. Finding no suitable anchorage or beach available, as both mainland and island were occupied by the Peloponnesian army and the harbour by their fleet, which showed no sign of coming out, he proceeded to the island of Proté, some eight miles to the north, and there passed the night. In the morning he returned, hoping that the enemy would come out to fight a battle in the open sea. But seeing no sign of that, and finding the enemy unprepared, with only part of his fleet manned and many men still on shore, he entered the Bay by both channels, dispersed the ships already formed up, pursued them to land, and attacked also those not yet manned. Much hand-to-hand fighting seems to have occurred. The defeat of the Peloponnesian fleet was complete, and thus the land force on Sphacteria was cut off and could be blockaded.[1] To permit of an embassy being sent to Athens to sue for peace an armistice was concluded. Its terms arranged for the provisioning of the garrison during the truce, and for the temporary surrender by the Lacedæmonians of about sixty ships.[2] The embassy failed and the truce ended, but the Athenians refused to return the ships in accordance with the terms of the armistice. Hostilities were resumed. The Athenian fleet, reinforced to seventy ships, strictly blockaded the island.[3] Nevertheless supplies continued to reach the garrison. The blockade promised to be protracted, and could not be maintained during the coming winter owing to the difficulty of supply and to the absence of a sheltered beach equal to the requirements of the ships' crews, upwards of fourteen thousand in number.[4] Demosthenes, the ruling spirit, seems to have determined that it was possible and necessary to carry the island by assault.[5] Influenced by Cleon, a political leader, who took the same view, the Athenians sent reinforcements under his command ; the allies in the west furnished others. When the preparations were complete, the whole of the army, perhaps five thousand men, and all the crews of the ships, except the lower tier of rowers, about ten thousand men, were landed, the defences were stormed and the survivors surrendered—292 in number, of

---

[1] Thu., iv. 13, 14.   [2] Ibid., iv. 16.   [3] Ibid., iv. 23.
[4] Ibid., iv. 26, 27.   [5] Ibid., iv. 29.

whom 120 were native Spartans, the original garrison having
been 420; the attendant helots are not included. These
Spartan prisoners belonged to the ruling class, and became
from henceforth an important asset in the hands of the
Athenians and a capital feature in the war. The blockade had
lasted seventy-two days, including the armistice of twenty
days.[1] Both armies now returned home, the Athenians leaving
a garrison in Pylus, not only to hold it but to raid and to
harry the surrounding country. These raids created unrest
among the helots, who formed the great mass of the population, and were disaffected and ready to desert or even revolt
if an opportunity offered.[2] Thus Pylus became not only a
base for the Athenian navy and privateers on that part of
the coast, but a centre of political unrest. Demosthenes at
Pylus, like Themistocles at Salamis, had occupied a position
which compelled attack. The Peloponnesians were forced
to risk a battle which resulted in the loss of their whole fleet
and secured the Athenian hold on the western trade route.
But we are to note that whereas Themistocles fixed the form
of the battle, Eurymedon had to accept that dictated by the
enemy, who could not be forced to fight on the open sea
against his will. The Pylus naval battle was of the "old
clumsy sort" which depended on hand-to-hand fighting rather
than on manœuvring. It indicated limitations to the "new
system" of tactics.

The Athenian policy of occupying positions off the enemy's
coast was now extended. Shortly after the fall of Sphacteria
the Methana peninsula north-east of the Peloponnesus was
captured and garrisoned.[3] In the following summer, 424,
the island of Cythera off the south coast was captured,[4] and
Nisæa, the seaport of Megara, was taken.[5] With Ægina,
which had been occupied early in the war,[6] Methana, Nisæa,
and the island of Salamis in her hands, Athens had full
control of the Saronic Gulf. No enemy trade could pass
through it. No food from over sea could reach Megara.
Moreover, the operations in the Bay of Pylus had secured
her preponderance in the western seas. Her ships, based
on Naupactus, blocked ingress to and egress from the Gulf

---

[1] Thu., iv. 31-39.   [2] Ibid., iv. 41.   [3] Ibid., iv. 45,
[4] Ibid., iv. 54.   [5] Ibid., iv. 69.   [6] Ibid., ii. 27.

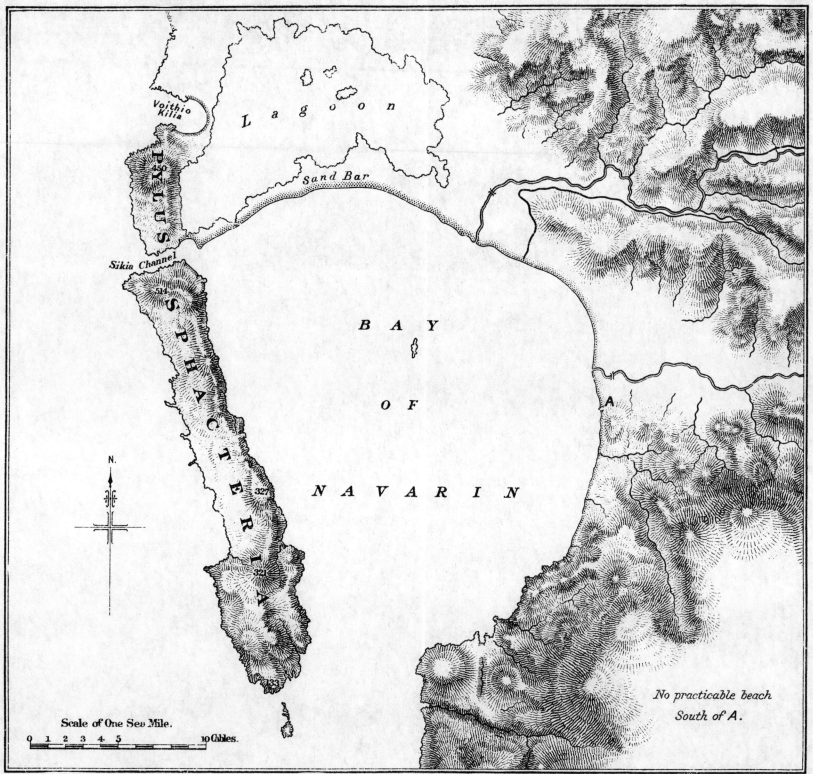

IX

Voithio
Kilia

PYLUS
450

L a g o o n

Sand Bar

Sikia Channel

514

S P H A C T E R I A

B A Y

O F

N A V A R I N

A

327

321

133

No practicable beach
South of A.

N.

Scale of One Sea Mile.

0 1 2 3 4 5   10 Cables.

Stanford's Geogl. Estabt, London.

of Corinth. The foreign sea-borne trade of Corinth must have been almost entirely stopped, and the wealth she derived from her carrying trade must have begun to dry up. According to Thucydides, Cythera was the port of call for merchant ships coming from Egypt;[1] he probably means ships bound to ports in Laconia and Messenia. Its possession, therefore, enabled Athens seriously to impede that trade. Hence, the Peloponnesus itself was now threatened with something in the nature of a sea blockade and a resulting shortage of imported food.

Henceforth the operations assumed a different character. On the one hand, the Peloponnesus was raided from Pylus, Cythera, and Methana, and a portion of the Peloponnesian army was thus held up.[2] On the other hand, the cross raids into Attica and the Megarid ceased,—on the part of the Peloponnesians, because the lives of the Spartan prisoners from Sphacteria would be forfeited if Attica were invaded; on the part of the Athenians, because operations against the city of Megara were undertaken and more extended ones in Bœotia were to follow. These new operations seem to have been largely due to the influence of Demosthenes, whose prestige had been increased by his recent successes. The expedition against Megara was sent seemingly before the summer solstice, in response to an invitation from a party in that city, but, owing to the intervention of Brasidas with a mixed army drawn from the Isthmus and from Bœotia, only succeeded in capturing Nisæa. The operations in Bœotia were arranged in conjunction with certain democratic exiles from the cities in that country; they included simultaneous invasions oversea from the Gulf of Corinth and by land from Attica.[3] The expedition by sea failed to effect a landing;[4] that by land suffered a severe defeat at Delium in the autumn and was driven back into Attica.[5] The attempt against Bœotia aimed at conquest, and was opposed to the advice given by Pericles; that against Megara cannot be so regarded, seeing that an Athenian hold of the Megarid would have cut the communications and covered the Athenian possessions in Thrace. The importance attached to these

[1] Thu., iv. 53.   [2] Ibid., iv. 55, 56.   [3] Ibid., iv. 76.
[4] Ibid., iv. 89.   [5] Ibid., iv. 96.

communications is shown by the Peloponnesian blockade and capture of Platæa early ·in the war,[1] and by the diversion in Thrace, now initiated by Brasidas on the invitation of Perdiccas, king of Macedonia, and of certain revolted Athenian tributary cities in Chalcidicé.[2]   The fall of Platæa had opened the most direct route from the Isthmus into Bœotia and to the north.   The diversion in Thrace was a counterstroke to the Athenian blockade of the Peloponnesus.

After relieving Megara, Brasidas, with a small Peloponnesian force, moved north, adroitly passed unopposed through Thessaly, then an ally of Athens, and joined Perdiccas before the autumnal equinox.[3]   The details of his operations do not concern us.   It is sufficient to say that Athens, being then heavily committed in Bœotia, did not send adequate reinforcements to Chalcidicé, and thus Brasidas was able to win over some Athenian tributary cities and to capture others. Among the latter was Amphipolis on the Strymon, which surrendered during the winter, after the bridge across the river had been surprised, and before the Athenian squadron from Thasus, some forty miles distant, could arrive with relief.[4]   Across this bridge passed the only road into eastern Thrace; above it Lake Cercinitis (Takhinos) blocked the way, below it the Athenian navy held the river.   Hence its importance.   This serious loss seems to have been due to some failure on the part of Thucydides, the officer in command of the squadron, and jointly responsible with the general at Amphipolis for the security of the Athenian position in Chalcidicé.   His banishment was the result.

Brasidas was now in a position to threaten the Hellespont and the Euxine corn trade, upon which Athens mainly relied. This trade seems to have passed by sea to Histiæa in northern Eubœa, an Athenian possession, thence by land to Eretria, whence it was shipped to Oropus and passed along the Deceleia road to Athens.[5]   The precise reasons for the land route through Eubœa are not known, but may have been the risks of navigation and the dangers from pirates. The direct route from the Hellespont to Attica involved a long stretch of open sea; the coasting route would have

[1] Thu., ii. 75-78 ; iii. 52.   [2] Ibid., iv. 79.   [3] Ibid., iv. 78.
[4] Ibid., iv. 106.   [5] Ibid., vii. 28.

included either the coast of Eubœa with its dangerous
possibilities as a lee shore, or the Eubœan channel with
its pirates from Locrian ports.[1] If Deceleia had been seized
and permanently held by a Peloponnesian garrison, this
route would have been closed and the trade would have
been forced to take the sea route round the Sunium
Promontory to Piræus and Athens.

We are to note that the aim of the diversion in Thrace,
as of the blockade of the Peloponnesus, was secondary. In
each case the action taken threatened not the armed forces,
but the resources on which the armed forces rested—viz., the
wealth, in the shape of tribute, and the corn supply of
Athens; the wealth-producing trade, the food supply, and
through the discontent of the helots, the man-power of the
Peloponnesus. Such was the effect resulting on either side
that in the following spring (423) a truce was arranged for
twelve months. Under its terms Athenian garrisons remained
in Pylus and the other positions on the Peloponnesian coast,
but all raids ceased and no deserters were received. Small
Peloponnesian rowing craft employed in the coasting trade
were free to put to sea, but none of their ships of war, and
presumably no sailing ships employed in the oversea trade,
were at liberty to leave port.[2]

During the truce all war operations ceased, except in
Chalcidicé, where they were continued by Brasidas. Reinforcements from Athens were sent there by sea,[3] but those
from the Peloponnesus, having to march by land, were
stopped by the Thessalians at the instigation of Perdiccas,
who had quarrelled with Brasidas and changed sides.[4] In
the following year (422) after the truce had ended, another
expedition was sent there by sea from Athens under the
command of Cleon.[5] The corresponding reinforcement from
the Peloponnesus was again stopped by the Thessalians.
Nevertheless, in the attempt made by Cleon to retake
Amphipolis the Athenians were defeated with heavy loss,
including their leader. At the same time fell Brasidas, the
most able Lacedæmonian commander produced by the war.
After the death of these two men no further military opera-

---

[1] Thu., ii. 32. [2] Ibid., iv. 117-119. [3] Ibid., iv. 129.
[4] Ibid., iv., 128, 132. [5] Ibid., v. 2.

tions were undertaken by either side, both being now inclined towards peace.

From the war had resulted no final military decision. The Peloponnesian army and the Athenian navy each remained still undefeated, but the Peloponnesians were suffering from the raids and the sea-blockade, while the Athenians feared further revolts of their tributary cities. After prolonged negotiations, extending through the autumn and winter, the so-called peace of Nicias was concluded in the spring (421), on the general principle that both sides should give up what they had gained by arms, including both territory and prisoners. The central conditions were that the Athenians should withdraw from the positions held by them on the coasts of the Lacedæmonian League, except Nisæa, the Peloponnesians from Chalcidicé, leaving the tributary cities to pay tribute to Athens, but otherwise independent. Athens was content with the terms; as also was Lacedæmon, but not her allies. These last were very discontented.[1] Although the war had lasted ten years, and had been the cause of much suffering and loss, the absence of a complete military defeat had left men unwilling to submit to the necessary sacrifices. Corinth was sore because she did not receive back Sollium and Anactorium;[2] Megara, because she did not regain Nisæa;[3] Bœotia, because she had to return Panactum, a frontier town, to Athens.[4] Moreover, the Chalcidians refused both to surrender Amphipolis to Athens, and to accept the terms of the treaty.[5]

[1] Thu., v. 17-20.   [2] Ibid., v. 30.   [3] Ibid., v. 17.
[4] Ibid., v. 18.   [5] Ibid., v. 21.

VIII.

THE OPERATIONS.

THE INTERMEDIATE PHASE, INCLUDING THE SYRACUSAN EXPEDITION.

IN consequence of the opposition to the terms of the peace of Nicias, Lacedæmon immediately concluded a treaty of alliance with Athens, and at the same time obtained the release of the Spartan prisoners taken at Sphacteria.[1] The other terms of the peace were only partially and never completely carried into effect. For example, on the one side the Chalcidicé cities continued their refusal to pay tribute,[2] and on the other the Athenians remained at Pylus.[3] The failure of her army to obtain a decision brought about by inability either to storm walled cities or to reduce them by blockade when in communication with the sea, the surrender at Sphacteria and the new alliance with Athens, had weakened Lacedæmon as the leading state in the Peloponnesus. War continued but assumed a new form, and became in the main a struggle between Lacedæmon and Argos for the leadership. During this confused phase Athens and Lacedæmon remained in alliance and ceased to invade each other's territory. Nevertheless Athens eventually sided with Argos. The operations were mainly confined to the Peloponnesus, and having been chiefly conducted on land need not be dwelt on. In the year 418 they culminated in the battle of Mantineia, where Lacedæmon and her allies defeated Argos, Athens, and others.[4] This victory restored the

---

[1] Thu., v. 23, 24.   [2] Ibid., vi. 10.   [3] Ibid., v. 115.
[4] Ibid., v. 70-74.

prestige of Lacedæmon and left her supreme on land as was Athens at sea.

The supremacy at sea, which Athens had maintained throughout the ten years' war, remained to her after the peace of Nicias. The use made of that supremacy during subsequent years was shown by the fleets sent to blockade Macedonia in 417,[1] to intervene in the affairs of Argos in 416, and to make the unprovoked attack on the island of Melos[2] which was captured in 416, the men of military age being put to death and the remainder of the inhabitants reduced to slavery. As Thucydides has argued with dramatic force, this attack was based on the principle that might gives right — that the stronger should rule the weaker without regard to anything but expediency and the self-interest of the stronger.[3] Such seems to have been during the culminating period of its ascendancy the ideal of the Athenian democracy, which was now led to embark on a new war while the old one was still undecided. The peace of Nicias had never been generally accepted; Lacedæmon was covertly hostile, and was still undefeated on land; with Corinth was open war; the Chalcidian cities were still in open revolt, and with them as with Bœotia was only an armistice terminable at ten days' notice. Under such conditions an expedition to Sicily was initiated. Its political object was nominally to aid certain cities which had applied to Athens for help against other cities, but really to conquer the island.[4] The vote authorising it was passed early in the spring of the year 415, and at the same time Alcibiades the son of Cleinias, Nicias the son of Niceratus, and Lamachus the son of Xenophanes were nominated as its commanders. Their instructions were to assist Egesta against Selinus; if this did not demand all their military strength, they were empowered to restore the Leontines, who had been dispossessed by the Syracusans, and generally to further as they deemed best the Athenian interests in Sicily.[5] Such instructions were not likely to lead to decided action, seeing that Alcibiades and Nicias were at variance about the political object, the former being strongly in favour of the conquest,[6] and the latter being

---

[1] Thu., v. 83. [2] Ibid., v. 84. [3] Ibid., v. 84-116.
[4] Ibid., vi. 1. [5] Ibid., vi. 8. [6] Ibid., vi. 15-18.

convinced that the expedition was contrary to the best interests of Athens,[1] while Lamachus had little influence on policy.

The Athenian fleet seems to have assembled at Corcyra towards the end of June, and to have numbered one hundred and thirty-four triremes, of which thirty-four belonged to allies and at least forty were transports. Thirty merchant ships and one hundred small vessels, all sailing ships using oars only as an auxiliary, were also pressed into the service, and a great number of other similar craft followed on their own account. The army included five thousand one hundred hoplites or heavy armed infantry, each of whom had one attendant, besides thirteen hundred light armed troops and thirty cavalry, or a total of eleven thousand five hundred and thirty, of whom the greater proportion were provided by allies of Athens.[2] These numbers must be taken as a minimum, since it is not certain that all the light armed troops are included. On this basis the total number of men in the fleet and army seems to have approached forty thousand, and it becomes clear that the expedition was a drain chiefly on the maritime resources of the Empire. Athens was about to divert her armed forces, which were chiefly maritime, to the conquest of territory—that is to say, to a war on land, which is the business of an army. It is important to examine the part played by the navy in this war of conquest, seeing that its primary rôle is to operate not on land but at sea against the enemy's armed ships. Pericles may have had this point in mind when, before the outbreak of the war, he warned his countrymen to confine their operations to the sea and not to extend their empire while they were at war, or to run into unnecessary dangers.[3] His advice really was not to pursue a political object which involved unsound military action—that is to say, a war on land with an insufficient army.

Meanwhile the Syracusans could not be persuaded that the Athenians would attack them. They made little preparation for defence and paid no heed to the statesman Hermocrates, the son of Hermon, whose advice was to send all available ships and two months' provisions to Tarentum,

---

[1] Thu., vi. 9-14.   [2] Ibid., vi. 43.   [3] Ibid., i. 143, 144.

where they would be in such a favourable position that the Athenian expedition would probably never leave Corcyra ?

His arguments, as reported by Thucydides, ran[1] :—

... "If all the Sicilian Greeks, ... taking two months' provisions, would put out to sea with all their available ships and prepare to meet the Athenians at Tarentum and the promontory of Iapygia, thereby proving to them that before they fight for Sicily they must fight for the passage of the Ionian Sea, we should strike a panic into them. They would then reflect that at Tarentum (which receive us), we, the advanced guard of Sicily, are among friends, and go forth from a friendly country, and that the sea is a large place not easy to traverse with so great an armament as theirs. They would know that after a long voyage their ships will be unable to keep in line, and coming up slowly and few at a time will be at our mercy. On the other hand, if they lighten their vessels and meet us in a compact body with the swifter part of their fleet, they may have to use oars, and then we shall attack them when they are exhausted. Or if we prefer not to fight, we can retire again to Tarentum. Having come over with slender supplies and prepared for a naval engagement, they will not know what to do on these desolate coasts. If they remain they will find themselves blockaded ; if they attempt to sail onwards they will cut themselves off from the rest of their armament, and will be discouraged ; for they will be far from certain whether the cities of Italy and Sicily will receive them. In my opinion the anticipation of these difficulties will hamper them to such a degree that they will never leave Corcyra."

Like the Athenians at Salamis, the Syracusans at Tarentum would have been on the flank of the enemy's advance and even more favourably placed in that on the Italian coast was no harbour, like Phalerum Bay, in which the Athenian armament could assemble to prepare for battle and to re·plenish its supplies after crossing the long stretch of open sea from Corcyra. Such a harbour was essential, if the Syracusan fleet was to be either fought or blockaded with any prospect of success, and without doing the one or the other the Athenian armament, including the large helpless convoy, could not pass.

During July the expedition left Corcyra, straggled across to the Iapygia promontory (Cape Sta. Maria di Leuca) and along the coast of Italy to Rhegium.[2] The plan of campaign

---

[1] Thu., vi. 34. Jowett's translation.   [2] Ibid., vi. 44.

had then to be settled. The faulty nature of the instructions under which the leaders acted now becomes apparent. Nicias proposed to limit their activities to what Egesta would pay for, or had promised to pay for, and to return home after Selinus was reduced; Alcibiades wished to win over allies before taking action to conquer the island; Lamachus alone gave the sound military advice to attack Syracuse at once, while the inhabitants were unprepared and the defences incomplete. Here are seen the political object and military action at issue. The former dominated the latter. The plan of Alcibiades was accepted,[1] but shortly afterwards that officer was recalled to Athens for political reasons, left his ship during the passage home, passed into exile, soon went over to the enemy, and was condemned to death in his absence.[2]

Henceforth the expedition was controlled by Nicias, who wasted six months in futile minor operations,[3] including a half-hearted attempt on Syracuse. During this interval the Syracusans strengthened their defences[4] and sent an embassy to ask for help from the Peloponnesians.[5] Corinth warmly supported their cause, and urged Lacedæmon not only to send help but to reopen the war with Athens.[6] Under the influence of Alcibiades, who met the embassy at Sparta, Lacedæmon agreed to send immediate aid to Sicily, aud appointed Gylippus, the son of Cleandridas, to command both the relieving expedition and the Syracusan forces, desiring him to make the necessary arrangements in co-operation with the Corinthian and Syracusan representatives.[7] The reopening of the war in Attica and the permanent occupation of Deceleia, which was much pressed by Alcibiades, were considered and postponed.

It was not until the spring—say March 414—that the Athenians moved from Catana, where they had wintered, to Thapsus, an anchorage about three sea miles north of Syracuse, and began the siege of that city.[8] The ancient Syracuse included both Ortygia and Achradina, and was pro-

[1] Thu., vi. 47-50.
[3] Ibid., vi. 62-72, 74, 94.
[5] Ibid., vi. 73.
[7] Ibid., vi. 93.

[2] Ibid., vi. 53, 61, 88.
[4] Ibid., vi. 75.
[6] Ibid., vi. 88.
[8] Ibid., vi. 97.

F

tected on the land side by a wall which ran north from the
Grand Harbour until it again reached the sea. West of
Achradina was an elevated tableland, called Epipolæ, which
ran inland upwards of four thousand yards from the city
wall, and rose from about 200 feet at Achradina to upwards
of 500 feet at an elevated position known as Euryalus. This
tableland was flanked to the south by the valley of the
Anapus, which was low-lying and marshy near the mouth of
the river. The Grand Harbour is about two sea miles long
from north to south by about one sea mile wide. The
entrance faces east, is about twelve hundred yards wide, and
is flanked by Ortygia to the north and a promontory called
Plemmyrium to the south. The lesser harbour lay between
Ortygia and Achradina, and seems to have been open to
the east (Plan XI.).

By the month of June the siege had made such progress
that the city was virtually cut off. Epipolæ had been seized ;
a fort had been erected there, and thence a wall had been run
almost to the Grand Harbour, to which the fleet was moved
to complete the investment on that side.[1] The wall intended
to be run north from the fort to the sea was still very incomplete, the call for it being less urgent as the lie of the
ground made the position strong against a sortie from the
city, although weak against attack by a relieving army, which
was not expected. About this time Lamachus was slain.
After his death less vigour began to be shown in the operations, but the chances of Athenian success continued to seem
favourable, and the Syracusans began to lose confidence,
since no help arrived from the Peloponnesus.[2] Presently
they were cheered by the arrival of a Corinthian trireme
with news that relief was at hand.[3]

In the same month of June Gylippus with the relieving
squadron was at Leucas. Alarmed by reports, all false, that
the investment of Syracuse was complete, he pushed with four
ships straight across to Tarentum, distant some two hundred
miles, leaving the remaining fifteen ships of his squadron to follow the usual coastwise route.[4] After much delay, due to bad
weather, he seems to have reached Locri, a city on the coast
of Italy some twenty miles north-east of the Herculis Promon-

---

[1] Thu., vi. 102. [2] Ibid., vi. 103. [3] Ibid., vii. 2. [4] Ibid., vi. 104.

tory (Cape Spartivento), where he heard that the investment of Syracuse was not yet complete, and that an army might still enter by way of Epipolæ.[1]   He had now to decide whether to proceed along the east coast of Sicily, risking a meeting with the Athenian fleet, and attempt to enter Syracuse by sea, or to pass through Siculum Fretum (Straits of Messina) and along the north coast to Himera, where he would be able to raise an army and with it march across the island and enter by land.   He chose the latter, slipped through the Straits before the ships sent by Nicias could intercept him, and on some uncertain date—probably in August—arrived with a small army on Epipolæ.   There he was joined by the Syracusans who marched out to meet him.[2]   It is sufficient to say of the subsequent operations, that after some fighting Gylippus ran a counter wall west from the city across Epipolæ to prevent the completion of the Athenian northern wall,[3] and on the high ground at the extremity of this counter wall he afterwards built a fort—Euryalus—to deny to others the route by which he himself had advanced.[4]   Thus his hold on Epipolæ, the key of the position, was secured, the Athenians were driven into the Anapus valley, much of which was swampy and unhealthy, their communications with the surrounding country were menaced, and the investment of the city was prevented.   Nicias had lost the initiative.   His land communications were seriously threatened by the garrison of Fort Euryalus and by the enemy's cavalry.   He found it necessary to occupy and to fortify Plemmyrium in order that he might be able to cover his supply ships, which, on entering the harbour, were flanked at short range by the enemy's fleet and reached him with difficulty.   To Plemmyrium he transferred his ships, the greater part of his stores, and a part of his army.   He was now on the defensive on land and was soon to be so at sea.   Presently the relieving Corinthian squadron arrived, having evaded the squadron sent by Nicias to intercept it on the coast of Italy.[5]   The Syracusans now manned a fleet and prepared to assume the offensive at sea. They had good prospects of success, since the Athenian fleet had much deteriorated; the efficiency of the crews had been

---

[1] Thu., vii. 1.   [2] Ibid., vii. 2.   [3] Ibid., vii. 4.
[4] Ibid., vii. 4.   [5] Ibid., vii. 1, 7.

destroyed and their number depleted by casualties on land,[1] by desertion, and by sickness; the ships had become sodden and foul by being constantly in the water, owing to want of opportunity to beach them. This deterioration, inseparable from such a service, promised to increase, whereas the Syracusan fleet, not being exposed to the same wear and tear, continued to gain strength and efficiency.[2]

It was now September. Both sides asked for reinforcements. Nicias reported to Athens that the expedition must be either withdrawn or reinforced by another large fleet and army. He also represented that another General should be sent to relieve him, as his health was bad. The Athenians do not seem to have realised that Nicias had failed as a leader. They did not release him from his command, but appointed as his colleagues Demosthenes, the son of Alcisthenes, and Eurymedon, the son of Eucles, the old colleagues of the Pylian campaign in 425, and nominated two officers already on the spot to act pending their arrival. They despatched Eurymedon in December with ten ships and a sum of money to Sicily, and directed Demosthenes to prepare an expedition to sail in the spring for the same destination.[3]

The Syracusans sent an embassy to Corinth and Lacedæmon, while Gylippus applied in person to the cities in Sicily.[4] Help in answer to these requests was forthcoming in two different ways. Indirect action was promised by Lacedæmon, who prepared to renew the war on land with Athens.[5] Direct aid was promised by the Peloponnesians, who prepared to send hoplites in merchant ships—*i.e.*, sailing ships—to Sicily. Corinth also manned a squadron

---

[1] " It has been and continues to be the ruin of our crews, that the sailors, having to forage and fetch water and wood from a distance, are cut off by the Syracusan horse, while our servants, since we have been reduced to an equality with the enemy, desert us. Of the foreign sailors, some . . . run off at once to the Silician cities; others . . . either find an excuse for deserting to the Syracusans, or they effect their escape into the country. . . ."—Thu., vii. 13. Nicias' despatch.

[2] " Our fleet was originally in first-rate condition: the ships were sound and the crews were in good order, but now, as the enemy are well aware, the timbers of the ships, having been so long exposed to the sea, are soaked, and the efficiency of the crews is destroyed. We have no means of drawing up our vessels and airing them, because the enemy's fleet is equal or even superior in numbers to our own, and we are always expecting an attack from them . . ."—Thu., vii. 12. Extract from Nicias' despatch.

[3] Thu., vii. 15, 16.   [4] Ibid., vii. 7.   [5] Ibid., vii. 18.

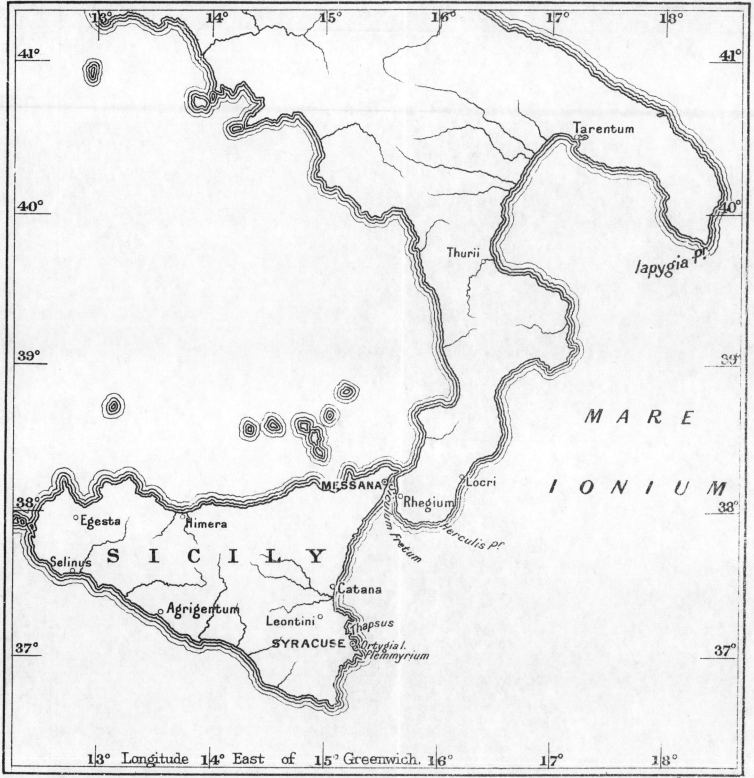

X

41°   13°   14°   15°   16°   17°   18°   41°

Tarentum

40°   40°

Thurii

Iapygia Pr.

39°   39°

MARE

IONIUM

Messana°   °Locri

38°   °Egesta   °Himera   °Rhegium   38°

Selinus   S I C I L Y   Siculum Fretum   Herculis Pr.

°Agrigentum   Catana

Leontini°   Thapsus

37°   SYRACUSE   Ortygia I.   37°
Plemmyrium

13° Longitude 14° East of 15° Greenwich. 16°   17°   18°

Stanford's Geogl. Estabt. London.

of twenty-five triremes to cover these transports from an
Athenian squadron of twenty triremes which had been
sent to intercept vessels sailing to Sicily from the Peloponnesus or Corinth. The latter squadron was based on
Naupactus.[1] The Sicilian cities furnished troops, who
accompanied Gylippus on his return to Syracuse in the
spring. Immediately after his return—say in April 413—
Gylippus arranged a simultaneous attack by the fleet and
army on the Athenian fleet and its base at Plemmyrium. At
sea eighty Syracusan triremes were defeated by sixty Athenian
in a battle which was fought partly inside and partly outside
the harbour. The losses were eleven to three; other details
are of no interest. On land the base at Plemmyrium was
captured with its large quantities of stores and supplies.
This was a severe blow to the Athenians.[2] With both sides
of the entrance in the hands of the enemy, ingress and egress
had to be fought for, which tended to confine their fleet inside
the harbour and to prevent supplies from coming in.[3]

The effect of constraining the Athenian fleet to remain
inside the harbour was twofold. Firstly, its activities at sea
were impeded, which exposed its supply ships to attack.
Thus, a Syracusan squadron of twelve triremes sailed shortly
after the battle under the command of Agatharcus. One of
these ships carried envoys to the Peloponnesus; the others
proceeded to the coast of Italy to raid the ships bringing
supplies from that country. Agatharcus was successful, but
on his return lost one ship to an Athenian squadron of twenty
ships watching for him off Megara Hyblæa, about ten miles
north of Syracuse.[4] Secondly, just as Themistocles at Salamis
forced a form of battle unfavourable to the Persians, so Gylippus
at Syracuse forced one unfavourable to the Athenians. All the
subsequent fighting took place inside the harbour and was of
"the old clumsy sort," in which superior speed gave no advantage and manœuvring had no place. After an interval of
some weeks, during which much desultory fighting occurred, a
great battle was joined—probably in July—in which eighty
Syracusan triremes defeated seventy-five Athenian.[5] It is
usual to attribute this Syracusan victory, as also the two sub-

[1] Thu., vii. 17.   [2] Ibid., vii. 21-23.   [3] Ibid., vii. 24.
[4] Ibid., vii. 25.   [5] Ibid., vii. 37-41.

sequent ones, to the strengthened beaks, already referred to, with which their ships were fitted. The real cause of the Athenian defeat seems to lie deeper, and to have been due to the opportunity given to use the beaks effectively. The military misuse of the Athenian fleet in the siege not only caused deterioration in ships and crews, but forced a battle in narrow waters involving a frontal attack. The sole hope of the Athenians now lay in Demosthenes and the relieving expedition.

Very early in the same spring—say early in April—Lacedæmon had redeemed her promise, and again begun open war with Athens. A Peloponnesian army under Agis, the son of Archidamus, the Lacedæmonian king, invaded Attica, fortified Deceleia, a town only fourteen miles from Athens on the direct route from Eubœa, and left a permanent garrison there.[1] Deceleia was made a centre whence both to ravage the country and to destroy the growing crops; also where runaway slaves sought refuge. Furthermore, it became an obstacle which prevented the import of food from Eubœa and the Euxine by the land route. Henceforth Athens was entirely dependent upon sea-borne supplies round Cape Sunium at greatly increased risk and cost.[2] The Athenians retaliated, at the beginning of spring while Deceleia was being fortified—say at the end of April—by sending a squadron of thirty ships under Charicles, the son of Apollodorus, to raid the coasts of the Peloponnesus, and to seize and garrison a fortified post in Laconia opposite Cythera as a raiding centre, a refuge for helot deserters, and a base for privateers operating against the Peloponnesian trade. They even diverted Demosthenes, who had assembled the relieving expedition at Ægina to assist Charicles, in the pursuit of these secondary military aims.[3] It was only after the post was established and after some appreciable delay, that Demosthenes proceeded on his voyage, while Charicles returned home. Parting company, probably on some date in May, Demosthenes steered up the west coast, touching at various points. On some uncertain date in June he was joined on the coast of Acarnania by Eurymedon, who had heard during his voyage from Sicily of the fall of Plemmy-

---

[1] Thu., vii. 19.   [2] Ibid., vii. 27, 28.   [3] Ibid., vii. 20.

rium, and brought the first news to Demosthenes of that
misfortune.[1] The joint commanders now detached ten
of their fastest ships to reinforce the Athenian squadron
at Naupactus, which shortly afterwards fought the indecisive
battle off Erineus,[2] as already narrated, with the Corinthian
squadron covering the sailing of the transports. These had
sailed at intervals during the spring, carrying some sixteen
hundred hoplites; some had started from ports inside the
Gulf of Corinth, others from ports outside—*e.g.*, Tænarus in
Laconia—just west of Cape Matapan.[3] The greater number
seem to have got away safely, but one is mentioned as having
been captured by Demosthenes at Phea in Elis.[4] Agatharcus
met one at Locri during his raid.[5] A number were driven by
stress of weather to the Libyan coast, along which they sailed
to Neapolis. Thence they crossed to Selinus, only reaching
Syracuse in August after the arrival of the relieving expedition and the culminating battle.[6]

From Acarnania the relieving expedition proceeded to
Corcyra, crossed to Italy, and slowly made its way along that
coast, gaining strength both in ships and men as it advanced.
After many delays, due to the need of raising reinforcements
at the various allied ports, perhaps also to adverse winds and
weather, and possibly to difficulty in procuring supplies for
such a large force, Demosthenes and Eurymedon reached
Syracuse in the month of July.[7] They entered the Grand
Harbour with a fleet, including foreign ships, of about
seventy-three triremes, carrying five thousand heavy armed
infantry of their own and of their allies, numerous light
armed troops, both Hellenic and Barbarian, and abundant
supplies, which means a numerous convoy of merchant ships.
The total number of men must have approached thirty
thousand.

According to Thucydides, Demosthenes at once saw that
the Syracusan counter wall, which prevented the investment
of the city, would be easily captured, if the high ground of
Epipolæ were taken and occupied. He resolved to make the
attempt. But before doing so the generals initiated minor
operations to regain superiority by sea and land, in which

[1] Thu., vii. 31.   [2] P. 39 *supra*.   [3] Thu., vii. 19.   [4] Ibid., vii. 31.
[5] Ibid., vii. 25.   [6] Ibid., vii. 50.   [7] Ibid., vii. 31, 33, 35, 42.

they succeeded, and made an attempt with engines on the counter wall which failed. The attack on Epipolæ now proceeded, and took place on a night "when the moon was bright."[1] This must have been about the end of July, when we know the moon was at the full, since the following full moon was eclipsed on the 27th August.[2] If allowance is made for the preliminary operations, the arrival of the fleet may be dated about the middle of the month. On this assumption Demosthenes took about three and a half months to proceed from Ægina to Syracuse, the distance run being about nine hundred sea miles. Of the battle for the heights of Epipolæ, it is sufficient to say that the Athenians were completely defeated. The operations on land had culminated, since the Athenians could not expect further reinforcements, whereas the Peloponnesian hoplites were at hand from Selinus, and all the Sicilian cities, except Agrigentum, had already united to strengthen Syracuse against Athens.[3]

All hope of reducing the city had to be abandoned. It was necessary to withdraw the army and the fleet before the latter was forced to fight under disadvantageous conditions inside the harbour. Both Demosthenes and Eurymedon seem to have fully realised the military dangers of the position, but Nicias was obdurate and refused to move.[4] The subsequent operations need not be dwelt on, since the result was a foregone conclusion. The Syracusans were reinforced. The Athenian fleet was defeated in two great battles inside the harbour, from which the exit was blocked by an obstruction before the latter of these was fought.[5] Their retreat by sea being cut off they attempted to withdraw by land, and in doing so the whole force was completely annihilated.[6]

The Syracusan expedition had ended in disaster, because its political object—to overrun and plunder the island— threatened the political freedom and security of the Greek world, whether in Sicily or elsewhere, thus evoking a general spirit of resistance. Furthermore, unsound military action was inseparable from the political object : the operations were ill conceived and feebly conducted, and the Athenian navy was misused.

---

[1] Thu., vii. 43, 44. [2] Ibid., vii. 50. [3] Ibid., vii. 33.
[4] Ibid., vii. 49. [5] Ibid., vii. 52, 56, 70. [6] Ibid., vii. 75-87.

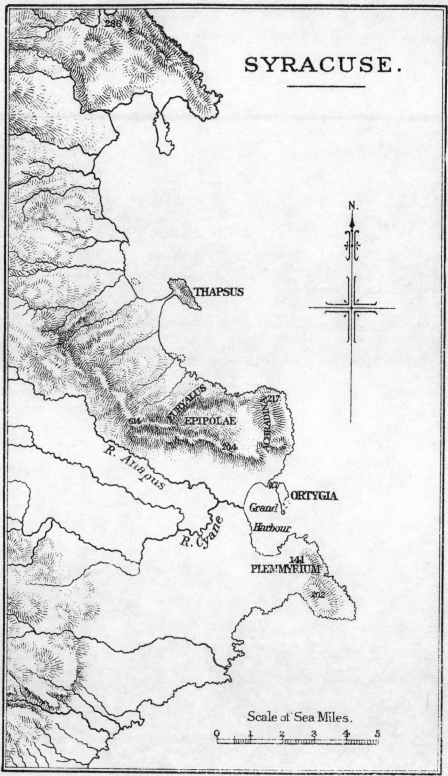

XI

SYRACUSE.

N.

THAPSUS

EURYALUS
614 ACHRADINA 217
EPIPOLAE
204

ca ORTYGIA
Grand
Harbour

R. Anapus

R. Cyane

141
PLEMMYRIUM
202

286

Scale of Sea Miles.

0 1 2 3 4 5

Stanford's Geog.l Estab.t London.

IX.

THE OPERATIONS.

THE WAR IN IONIA.

THE destruction at Syracuse of more than two hundred Athenian triremes and their highly trained and skilled crews —the armed force upon which the Athenian Empire floated— changed the character of the war. The ten years' war was indecisive, because the principal armed forces on either side —the Athenian Navy and the Lacedæmonian Army—did not and could not come into direct collision. To reach a complete decision by land and sea, either the Empire must raise an army strong enough to meet the League on land, which was beyond the power of Athens owing to the nature of her Empire, or the League must raise a navy strong enough to meet the Empire at sea, which became possible after the disaster at Syracuse. The war in Ionia, as the new phase is commonly called, became decisive, because ultimately the League concentrated on the primary military aim — the destruction of the Athenian fleet—whereas during the earlier years of the war secondary military aims predominated. On the one side, the Empire no longer blockaded the Peloponnesus and stopped its trade with the same efficiency. On the other side, the League not only permanently held and ravaged Attica, and stopped the transit trade by the Deceleia route, which was not done during the ten years' war, but gave more effective aid to the revolting tributary cities of Athens, and even threatened her over-sea trade.

The first signs of the changed conditions were seen during the winter (413-12) following the disaster at Syracuse in the

efforts on both sides to build triremes, of which the League
laid down one hundred;[1] in the Athenian withdrawal from
the fortified post in Laconia, whence they had harried the surrounding country and the sea-borne trade;[2] in the fortifications
erected on the Sunium Promontory to protect the Athenian
corn ships on their way from Eubœa and the Euxine to Athens;
in the overtures to the League from the Persian Satraps,
Tissaphernes at Sardes in Lydia and Pharnabazus in Hellespontine Phrygia, also from Eubœa, Lesbos, Erythræ, and
Chios, who were anxious to revolt.[3] Defeat made apparent
the political weakness of the Athenian Empire. Having
previously determined that Chios really had a fleet of sixty
triremes, the League entered into alliance with her and
agreed to assist the revolt of the cities in Ionia.[4] Their plan
was to send a fleet to Chios in the first place, then to work
north to Lesbos with the Hellespont as the final goal,[5] the
aim being to encourage revolts in the Athenian tributary
cities of that region and to stop the corn trade from the
Euxine. The negotiations seem to have been completed
before the vernal equinox. In pursuance of the plan, twenty-
one of the thirty-nine triremes belonging to the League at
the Isthmus were transported during the spring across it
and moved to Cenchreæ. After the Isthmian games[6] in the
year 412 the Athenians began to suspect the Chians of an
intention to revolt, and shortly constrained them to send
seven ships to join the Athenian fleet as a pledge of fidelity
to the alliance. Furthermore, as the Athenian aim was to
prevent the Peloponnesians crossing the Ægean to Ionia, the
ships at Cenchreæ were watched and, when they attempted
to proceed to Chios, were turned back by an Athenian
squadron. After an interval Alcamenes, with the twenty-one
triremes, made a second attempt, but was met by a fleet of
thirty-seven—including seven Chian—and driven back with
the loss of one ship into Spiræum (Port Franco), a harbour
about six miles east of Cenchreæ. There his ships were
attacked not only on the water but also on the beach. Most
of them were damaged and he himself was slain. On the
morrow a Peloponnesian land force arrived to protect the

---

[1] Thu., viii. 3. [2] Ibid., viii. 4. [3] Ibid., viii. 5, 6. [4] Ibid., viii. 6.
[5] Ibid., viii. 8. [6] The exact date of the Isthmian games is uncertain.

ships, which were then drawn high up on the beach. The attack could not be again renewed without the help of an army, because the number of *epibatai* or marines carried by the ships was very small and the rowers were unarmed. The land defence was stronger than the sea attack. Ships alone were then, as often since, unequal to the attack on a land position. The Athenians were obliged to watch the Peloponnesians, basing their squadron on an island, not named by Thucydides, but evidently the modern Hevræo, distant rather over a mile, where they encamped. The conditions were unfavourable for the watchers, since the harbour of Spiræum permitted the rapid exit of the watched with a minimum of delay, and the island base was so near that only very short warning of an impending attack could be given. As a consequence, after an interval of some weeks, the twenty Peloponnesian ships made a sortie, defeated the Athenian squadron of equal number, took four ships and got away to Cenchreæ, where they found Astyochus the Lacedæmonian who was about to assume command of the Peloponnesian fleet.[1] The incident is not only typical of the conditions which militate against success in maintaining a watch on an enemy's fleet, but is an early example of the influence exercised by the land on the conduct of war at sea. Strong positions, in which the weaker fleet can make a stand against the stronger, are to be found only on the coast and not on the ocean. Such positions vary in strength from those which provide complete immunity from attack by ships, as in this case, to those which give only some advantage to the defending over the attacking ships, as was given to Polyanthes over Diphilus at Erineus.[2] In neither case is the weaker fleet permanently withdrawn from the war; it usually remains ready to issue, and waits a more favourable opportunity; it is on the defensive. The stronger fleet watches more or less closely according to circumstances, and remains ready to fight, or accepts the disadvantage and attacks; it is on the offensive.

This military watch[3] with its primary aim to fight must

---

[1] Thu., viii. 10-20.   [2] P. 39, *supra.*

[3] Cf. The military watch of Cornwallis off Brest in 1803 and following years, and of Togo off Port Arthur in 1904.

be distinguished from the commercial blockade[1] with its
secondary aim to stop the trade, which Athens had enforced
but now relaxed over the southern trade route. The distinc-
tion is none the less important in that the two operations are
sometimes blended, as was seen about this time when an
Athenian squadron of twenty-seven ships on the western
trade route intercepted off Leucadia an enemy's squadron of
sixteen returning home from Sicily and captured one, the
remainder getting away to Corinth.[2]

A second expedition of five ships under the Spartan
Chalcideus, with whom was Alcibiades, sailed from Laconia
for Chios immediately after Alcamenes had been turned back.[3]
An Athenian squadron of eight ships, under Strombichides,
the son of Diotimus, from the force off Spiræum, was detached
in pursuit, but failing to overhaul them returned instead of
following to Ionia as was required in view of the attitude of
Chios and of the value of time.[4] Taking every precaution
to conceal their own movements and the check to Alcamenes,
Chalcideus and Alcibiades proceeded first to Corycus, a port
on the mainland about twenty-five miles south-east of Chios,
and thence sailed with so little delay that their arrival at
Chios was a surprise to the inhabitants. The island at once
revolted from Athens. They now had fifty-three Chian
triremes — seven were with the squadron off Spiræum and
were now withdrawn and disarmed by the Athenians—in
addition to their own five, and their object was to spread the
revolt. Erythræ, on the mainland opposite, and Clazomenæ,
in the Gulf of Smyrna, ere long followed the example of Chios.
As soon as the revolt at Chios was known at Athens, orders
were given to man a large number of ships; also a decree was
passed sanctioning the use of the money specially reserved
nineteen years earlier to meet an emergency and all that
remained of the accumulated wealth of Athens.[5] Furthermore, Strombichides with eight ships was sent to Samos,
which being centrally placed in Ionia at the eastern end of
the shortest and safest route for triremes across the Ægean

---

[1] Cf. The commercial blockade of the South during the American Civil War of
1861-5.

[2] Thu., viii. 13.

[3] Ibid., viii. 12.

[4] Cf. Nelson's pursuit of Villeneuve.

[5] Thu., viii. 14, 15.

from Athens, became the base of the Athenian squadrons. He could do no more than check revolts. With that object he first went with nine ships, including one Samian, to Teos, a city midway between Chios and Samos, which are about seventy sea miles apart, but was driven back to Samos by Chalcideus and Alcibiades with twenty-three ships supported by a land force from Clazomenæ and Erythræ, which was admitted to Teos and destroyed the fortifications. Chalcideus and Alcibiades then returned to Chios, where they armed and landed their own crews, replacing them with Chians. They next moved with twenty-five ships, including their own five, to Miletus, distant about eighty sea miles to the south-east of Chios, instead of going north to Lesbos in accordance with the original plan. On arrival they were admitted by the Milesians who at once revolted from Athens. Strombichides, at Samos, flanking their line of advance, failed to intercept them, but followed in close pursuit with nineteen ships, including twelve under Thrasycles who had recently joined from Athens. Admittance to Miletus being refused, he anchored his squadron at the island of Lade, opposite the city, and remained to watch Chalcideus, who made no attempt to fight, and was reduced to inactivity notwithstanding his superiority in numbers.[1]

These operations call for two remarks. Strombichides, as soon as he was strong enough, struck at the enemy's armed ships, showing that his mind was dominated by the military object; whereas Chalcideus, under the political influence of Alcibiades, did no more than foster and spread revolt with a view to weakening the resources of Athens. The treaty of alliance now negotiated at Miletus by Chalcideus on behalf of the Lacedæmonian League with Tissaphernes for the Persian king, emphasised the same policy.[2] That instrument recognised the Greek cities in Ionia as possessions of the king, and the contracting parties agreed to prevent the payment of tribute to Athens by the cities.

Furthermore, a Peloponnesian fleet of triremes from the Laconian Gulf crossing the Ægean to free Chalcideus, had the choice of three routes—the northern, *via* Melos, Myconus, Icaria, taken by Alcidas[3] in the year 427; the central, *via*

[1] Thu., viii. 15-17.   [2] Ibid., viii. 18.   [3] P. 53 *supra*.

Melos, Ios, Amorgos, and Leros; the southern, *viâ* Crete, Carpathus, and the Sporades. The Athenians based on Samos were favourably placed to watch Chalcideus at Miletus, to cover their own detachments in Chian waters, and to prevent the advance of any such fleet to Lesbos and the Hellespont.

The Chians, left to their own resources, now sent ten ships to draw into revolt certain cities on the mainland north of Samos. These ships were sighted not far from Lebedos and dispersed by a squadron of sixteen ships under Diomedon, who was bringing this further reinforcement from Athens. One ship fled to Ephesus, five reached Teos, and four were forced on shore and captured without the crews, who landed and escaped. Diomedon then proceeded to Samos, where a revolution shortly afterwards occurred, and transferred power from the oligarchs to the democrats, who favoured the Athenian alliance.[1] Further raids by both sides on the mainland cities in this region gave no marked results.

About the time of the Peloponnesian sortie from Spiræum,[2] the principal operations in Ionia were moved to Lesbos. The Chians sent an expedition of thirteen ships to that island, where they brought about revolts at Methymna on the north coast and at Mitylene on the east. Shortly afterwards another Athenian reinforcement of ten ships joined Diomedon at Samos and the Lacedæmonian Astyochus with four ships arrived at Chios from Cenchreæ. The disposition of the naval forces at that time seems to have been :—

	Athenian.	Peloponnesian.	Chian.	Total.
At Miletus	20	5	20	= 25[3]
At Methymna in Lesbos .	—	—	4 }	
At Mitylene　　" .	—	—	9 }	= 13[4]
At Chios. . . .	—	4	16[5]	
At Samos	26	—	—	
	46	9	49[6]	

Three days after the arrival of Astyochus at Chios, Leon and Diomedon with twenty-five ships passed through the

[1] Thu., viii. 19-21.　　[2] P. 79 *supra.*　　[3] Ibid., viii. 16, 17.
[4] Ten were taken by Leon and Diomedon, viii. 22, 23.
[5] Apparently unmanned.
[6] Seven more were in the hands of the Athenians, and four had been taken by Diomedon (viii. 19), making 60 in all.

Chios Channel steering north for Lesbos. On the same evening Astyochus left Chios with five ships, including one Chian, for Pyrrha in the same island, and distant fifty-four sea miles. That place lies ten sea miles up an arm of the sea, which can be entered only through one narrow channel. There he was in a *cul-de-sac* and liable to be destroyed or shut in. It was probably to avoid such a misfortune that he moved on the day following his arrival to Eresus on the south coast, where he heard that the Athenians, on reaching Mitylene—distant fifty sea miles from Chios—had at once entered the harbour, captured the nine Chian ships lying there, landed, defeated the Mitylenæans and taken possession of the city. Astyochus was shortly joined by three ships from Methymna, the fourth having fallen into the hands of the enemy. He had now only eight ships including four Chian, and was clearly outmatched at sea. After some futile minor operations he withdrew to Chios, leaving the Athenians predominant in Lesbos and free to press and secure the return of Clazomenæ to their alliance.[1]

After an interval Astyochus was joined by a reinforcement from Cenchreæ of six ships which raised the Peloponnesian numbers present with him to ten, but the Athenian Navy still remained predominant. Leon and Diomedon, basing their ships on islands in the Chios Channel and on fortified posts on the adjacent mainland, not only pressed the Chians by sea, but landed and drove them inside their walls. The Athenian efforts to obtain a decision failed because the Chian walls were impregnable and surrender could not be forced by ravaging their country, although the resulting hardships were so great that a disaffected party threatened to carry over the city to the Athenians.[2]

Towards the end of the summer (412) the principal operations began to centre round Miletus, where some weeks earlier Chalcideus had been killed in a skirmish, but Strombichides' squadron still remained watching. Presently—say about the equinox—an Athenian fleet of forty-eight triremes, of which some were transports, arrived at Samos under the command of Phrynichus, Onomacles, and Scironides. On board were one thousand Athenian hoplites, fifteen hundred Argives, and

---

[1] Thu., viii. 23.　　　　　[2] Ibid., viii. 24.

one thousand of the allies. Although not so stated, it is probable that the fleet was attended by a convoy of merchant
ships as victuallers. The expedition crossed over to Miletus,
landed and fought a battle with a mixed force of Milesians,
Peloponnesians, from the squadron of Chalcideus, and mercenaries of Tissaphernes, who was there in person. After the
battle the Milesians withdrew within the city, and in the
ordinary course would have been presently walled in. On
the very same afternoon Phrynichus received intelligence
that a combined fleet of fifty-five ships—thirty-three Peloponnesian and twenty-two Sicilian—under Therimenes the Lacedæmonian, either had been, or then actually was, at Leros,
distant about thirty-five sea miles from Miletus. He seems
to have had present with him at this time about sixty-eight
triremes—if the twenty in the watching squadron are included
—but some of his ships were only fitted as transports, and
therefore unfit for battle. Moreover, the twenty-five ships
of Chalcideus were still at Miletus. Being outnumbered, he
insisted, in the face of strong opposition, as is stated by
Thucydides, on embarking the army at once and returning to Samos. The whole fleet sailed the same evening, and
shortly afterwards the Argive contingent withdrew from the
expedition and returned home.[1]

While the Athenians were withdrawing, Alcibiades, who
had taken part in the battle before Miletus, was riding to
Teichiussa, a port in the Iasian Gulf due east thirty-five to
forty sea miles from Leros. There he arrived the same night,
found Therimenes and gave him the first news of the battle.
Urged by Alcibiades to relieve Miletus, Therimenes sailed at
dawn for that port, distant nearly forty sea miles, and on
arrival found that the Athenians had left.[2] The reader is
asked to consider the opportunity, apparently missed by
Therimenes, in proceeding from Leros to Teichiussa instead
of going direct to Miletus with the intention to attack the
Athenians, who, as he had learnt, were then at that place.

The ships at Miletus now joined Therimenes, raising his
number to about eighty. After a stay of one day he returned
to Teichiussa to pick up the masts and sails landed there in
preparation for battle. Pressed by Tissaphernes, who had

[1] Thu., viii. 25, 27.　　　　　　[2] Ibid., viii. 26, 28.

promised to provide the money to pay the fleet, he now joined him in a surprise attack on the city of Iasus, which was plundered and left in Persian hands. The allied fleet returned about the end of September to Miletus, which became its headquarters, and shortly afterwards received one month's pay from Tissaphernes.[1]

The withdrawal of the expedition from Miletus was not the only result produced by the arrival of the allied fleet under Therimenes in Ionian waters. The Athenian squadron in Chian waters also fell back on Samos. Thus the operations against Chios were abandoned, Astyochus was left free to put to sea, and Lesbos free to revolt. Furthermore, the Athenians not only concentrated, but increased the strength of the fleet to one hundred and four ships by a reinforcement of thirty-five ships from Athens under Charminus, Strombichides, and Euctemon.[2] On the other side, Astyochus made no immediate effort to concentrate. With twenty ships, including ten Chian, he raided Clazomenæ and other places — say in October—but without any success. After much delay, due to bad weather and strong winds, to which the trireme was very susceptible, he returned to Chios. He was only prevented from intervening in Lesbos by the weakness of his own force and by the refusal of assistance by Pedaritus, the newly-appointed Lacedæmonian Governor of Chios, who arrived a few days later, having marched round from Miletus, where he had been landed by Therimenes with an escort of Greek mercenaries from Iasus. It was probably not until quite early in November that he sailed with about ten Peloponnesian ships for Miletus to assume the command of the allied fleet, to which he had been appointed. The delay in doing so seems to indicate that he relied on political rather than military action—on raising revolts in the tributary cities rather than on taking action with the fleet, the real controlling factor in the war.[3]

About the same time as the operations of Astyochus in Chian waters, an allied squadron of twelve Laconian, Syracusan, and Thurian ships under Dorieus, the son of Diagoras, reached Cnidus, which had already revolted from Athens. These ships were not added to the main allied fleet at Miletus,

---

[1] Thu., viii. 28, 29.   [2] Ibid., viii. 30.   [3] Ibid., viii. 31-33.

G

but were used, as to one half, to protect the city of Cnidus, as to the other half, to cruise off the neighbouring Triopium Promontorium (C. Crio) against the passing trade from Egypt. The cruising six, being only sixty-five sea miles from Samos, were captured by an Athenian detachment from the main fleet, which also attacked Cnidus, but without success, and then returned to Samos.[1]

Meanwhile the Athenian fleet was reorganised and fresh dispositions were made. One division of seventy-four ships remained at Samos; another of thirty ships under Strombichides, Onomacles, and Euctemon, accompanied by transports with troops, sailed for Chian waters and narrowly missed Astyochus on his way to Miletus. The two squadrons anchored on the same night on either side of the Corycus promontory without either being aware that the other was so near. An encounter was only avoided by an unexpected call to Astyochus to return to Erythræ for a conference with the Governor of Chios; that done, he again sailed for Miletus.[2] Strombichides continued his voyage and finally reached Lesbos, having lost three ships during the passage in a gale of wind, which forced the remainder to seek temporary refuge at Phœnicus, a port on the eastern side of the Chios Channel. Shortly afterwards he crossed over and established his troops in a fortified post at Delphinium, a port on the coast not far from the city of Chios.[3] Delphinium became a centre, like Deceleia in Attica, whence the country was ravaged and supplies cut off, and where runaway slaves were received. The inhabitants of the city were threatened with such great privations that Pedaritus was driven to apply for relief to Astyochus, who either would not or could not help him.

On arriving at Miletus and taking over the command, Astyochus found the allied fleet abundantly supplied and the payment of the troops formally undertaken by the Persian king in a revised treaty concluded with Tissaphernes by Therimenes.[4] If to the original twenty-five ships of Chalcideus are added the fifty-five of Therimenes and the ten under Astyochus himself, the number present there

[1] Thu., viii. 35.
[2] Ibid., viii. 30, 33.
[3] Ibid., viii. 34, 38.
[4] Ibid., viii. 36.

becomes ninety, against which the Athenians had seventy-four at Samos without counting the six recently captured off the Triopium Promontory. Both sides had detachments. On the part of the allies were at Cnidus the six ships of Dorieus and in the north seventeen Chian ships, these last being faced by twenty-seven Athenian. Notwithstanding his numerical superiority Astyochus remained inactive when Pedaritus asked for help, and the Athenian fleet under Phrynichus and Scironides made threatening movements from Samos, as now happened.[1]

While the main fleets were thus inactive at Samos and Miletus respectively, and Chios was pressed—say in December 412—a Peloponnesian squadron of twenty-seven ships under the command of Antisthenes, a Spartan, surprised an Athenian squadron of ten ships at Melos and destroyed three, the crews escaping. The remaining seven ships got away and carried the news to Samos. This Peloponnesian squadron had been fitted out at the instigation of Pharnabazus for service at the Hellespont. On board were eleven Spartan commissioners, who were authorised to send on such ships as they saw fit from Miletus to the Hellespont under the command of Clearchus, the son of Ramphias; they were further empowered to act as advisers to Astyochus, or even to supersede him by appointing Antisthenes in his stead should the necessity arise. Fearing that he might be intercepted if the central route were followed, Antisthenes now took the southern one, *via* Crete, and seems to have reached Caunus, a port in Caria, nearly seventy sea miles east of Cnidus, towards the end of the year 412.[2] As soon as the arrival of Antisthenes at Caunus and his request for an escort became known at Miletus, Astyochus abandoned any idea he may have entertained of relieving Chios, and put to sea to join Antisthenes, leaving some ships to protect Miletus.[3]

On his passage he raided and plundered the city of Cos, some forty-five miles south of Miletus; thence he sailed fifteen miles to Cnidus, where he arrived after dark and learned that Charminus with twenty Athenian ships from Samos was cruising off the island of Symè, some twenty-

[1] Thu., viii. 38.   [2] Ibid., viii. 39.   [3] Ibid., viii. 40, 41, 61.

five miles to the eastward, to intercept Antisthenes. He at once pushed on. Owing to thick weather his ships straggled during the night and at dawn were much dispersed. The Athenians, thinking that the ships at first sighted were from Caunus, attacked, sank three and disabled others, but finding their mistake when the main body came up they fled, lost six ships during the pursuit, and finally reached Halicarnassus. After the action Astyochus returned to Cnidus, where he was joined by Antisthenes. The allied fleet on the coast of Ionia now numbered one hundred and thirty-seven,[1] of which ninety-four were with Astyochus and the remainder either at Miletus or Chios. Immediately after the junction the united fleet made an excursion to Symè, and returned immediately.[2]

As soon as the news of the action reached Samos the Athenian fleet sailed for Symè, and was probably joined off Cos by Charminus and his detachment from Halicarnassus, which raised its numbers to eighty-one.[3] Thus, with the twenty-seven ships in Chian waters, the Athenian strength in Ionia was now one hundred and eight. At Symè they embarked the masts and sails left behind by Charminus, called at Loryma, a port on the mainland about ten miles

[1] Chian squadron 60
    Less handed over to Athens 7
    Captured off Lesbos and by Diomedon . . 16
    — 23

    37
Chalcideus' squadron 5
Therimenes' ,, ... 55
Astyochus' ,, ... 10
Dorieus' ,,   12, less 6 captured . . . 6
Antisthenes' ,, ... 27

    140
    Less sunk off Symè 3

    137
[2] Thu., viii. 41, 42.
[3] From Samos 54
Charminus' squadron, 20, less 6 lost . . . 14
Captured off Cape Triopium 6
Melos' squadron, 10, less 3 burnt 7

    81

east of Symè and then returned to Samos.[1] They must have
passed not far from Cnidus, but Astyochus made no attempt
to attack, although he was superior in numbers. He may
have been occupied in repairing the damages received by
his ships in the recent fight, but his inaction may have been
due to other causes, which require to be shortly explained.

After the death of Chalcideus and the defeat at Miletus
Alcibiades became discredited in Lacedæmon, whence orders
for his execution were issued to Astyochus. To save his
life he passed over to Tissaphernes—say in October 412—
and began to intrigue. On the one hand, he counselled
Tissaphernes to withhold supplies and to reduce payments
to the allies in order to weaken them, also to bribe their
leaders and to promise the help of the Phœnician fleet
without intending to give it, in order to delay a decision by
battle. This policy tended to prolong the war and to wear
out both sides, which was to the interest of the Persian king.
On the other hand, he suggested to the Athenians at Samos
that the form of government at Athens should be changed
from a democracy to an oligarchy. Furthermore, he encouraged them, in the event of an oligarchy being set up,
to expect help from Tissaphernes, although there seems to
have been no intention to give it.[2]

Persian influence seems to have been dominant in the
allied fleet during its stay at Miletus, and until its arrival at
Cnidus and the conference there between Tissaphernes and
the Spartan Commissioners, headed by Lichas, the son of
Arcesilaus. The Commissioners took exception to the
Persian claims to power over Greek cities in Europe and the
islands which had been admitted in the treaty concluded by
Chalcideus and implied in that arranged by Therimenes.
They would not have the fleet maintained by Persia on such
terms. Angry at this opposition, Tissaphernes left without
settling anything.[3] Having quarrelled with Tissaphernes, and
desiring to be independent of his financial aid, the allies now
accepted an invitation from the leading men of Rhodes, and
moved their whole fleet to that island—probably before the
middle of January 411. Shortly afterwards the island
revolted from Athens. There they collected a considerable

---

[1] Thu., viii. 43.   [2] Ibid., viii. 45, 46.   [3] Ibid. viii. 43.

sum of money to pay the fleet, also without doubt supplies of food, otherwise they remained inactive for eleven weeks—say until the end of March—notwithstanding that the Athenians made descents on the island, and even based their fleet on the adjacent island of Chalcè.[1]

During the same period the Athenian oligarchs, headed by Pisander, pushed the intrigues at Samos and Athens to overthrow the democracy. When these were completed—say in February—Pisander crossed over into Asia to claim the expected help from Tissaphernes, but Alcibiades made on his behalf such exorbitant demands that Pisander was driven to break off the negotiations.[2] Tissaphernes had severed his relations with both sides, but wishing to preserve an even balance between them, and fearing that a starving fleet might raid and plunder the littoral cities of his satrapy, he not long afterwards made up his quarrel with the allies, concluded a new treaty more favourable to them, furnished them with supplies, agreed to maintain their fleet under certain conditions, and spoke of bringing up the Phœnician fleet to co-operate.[3]

It will be seen that the difficulties in providing money and food for the large number—perhaps twenty thousand or more —of men in the allied fleet were exploited by Tissaphernes and Alcibiades to influence its movements. The need for military action had hitherto remained in the background, but now came forward. The news from Chios had been gradually becoming more serious. A sortie of the whole garrison had been defeated, Pedaritus had been slain, and the inhabitants were suffering severely from famine. A new Governor, the Spartan Leon, with a mixed allied squadron of twelve ships, had been sent there from Miletus. Not long after his arrival —say in March 411—the Chians pressed by famine had made another sortie, and had fought an indecisive action with thirty-six allied against thirty-two Athenian triremes, in which the allies had some advantage. Nevertheless Chios was still pressed and additional help was needed.[4] Furthermore, the mission of the allied fleet in the south had been to some extent completed by the revolt of Rhodes and Cnidus, whereas

---

[1] Thu., viii. 44.
[2] Ibid., viii. 48-54, 56.
[3] Ibid. viii. 57, 58.
[4] Ibid., viii. 55, 56, 61.

the original allied plan of operations in the Hellespontine region still remained to be executed. With the immediate object of relieving Chios, the allied fleet left Rhodes for Miletus, probably at the end of March. At the same time the Athenian fleet sailed from Chalcè for Samos. The two fleets sighted each other off the Triopium Promontory, but no attack was made by either side. On arrival at their respective destinations the Athenians still flanked the allied line of advance to Chios, which caused Thucydides to make the comment: "The Lacedæmonians now saw that they could no longer relieve Chios without a battle at sea."[1]

About this time, the operations at sea were influenced by a diversion effected by a small land force under Dercyllidas, a Spartan, which marched along the coast to the Hellespont and brought about revolts against Athens at Abydus and Lampsacus. As soon as the news reached Strombichides he left Chian waters with twenty-four Athenian triremes, some of which were transports with troops, retook Lampsacus, failed at Abydus, and placed a garrison in Sestus. The departure of Strombichides left the Athenians inferior in Chian waters, whereupon Astyochus proceeded there with two ships, broke the sea blockade of Chios, brought away the allied ships, and with his united forces—probably greatly superior in number—offered battle to the Athenian fleet at Samos. The Athenians did not accept battle, but waited a more favourable opportunity. Astyochus returned to Miletus.[2]

Meanwhile the intrigues of Alcibiades were bearing fruit. Before the fleets moved north from Rhodian waters, the democracy at Athens had been overturned by the oligarchist Four Hundred, but the corresponding movement at Samos had been suppressed.[3] Now the Athenian armament at Samos openly declared itself against the oligarchy at Athens, and replaced those of its leaders as were oligarchist by well-known steadfast democrats, such as Thrasyllus and Thrasybulus.[4] It did not move to Athens to overthrow the oligarchy, but adhered to its primary rôle and remained at its post, ready to destroy or to neutralise the action of the enemy's armament. Thus, Ionia was covered, and Athens

---

[1] Cf. Themistocles before Salamis, *supra*, p. 26.
[2] Thu., viii. 61-63.   [3] Ibid., viii. 65-70   [4] Ibid., viii. 75, 76.

was saved from civil war and left free to work out its own
political salvation. But this decision was only reached after
much agitation and discussion, and, according to Thucydides,
was largely due to the influence of Alcibiades.[1]

Furthermore, discontent reigned among the crews of the
allied fleet at Miletus. Their complaints were that Astyochus
had neglected favourable opportunities to fight, and that
Tissaphernes had withheld or reduced payments and had
failed to bring up the Phœnician fleet.[2] Under this pressure
Astyochus again left Miletus—perhaps in May—with one
hundred and twelve ships for Mycale[3]—a position on the
mainland about three miles from Samos—where the local
land forces also mustered. Thence the Athenians with
eighty-two ships had just withdrawn to Samos, where they
awaited the arrival of Strombichides, who had been recalled
with his squadron from the Hellespont. On hearing that
Strombichides had rejoined, Astyochus gave up his intended
attack on Samos, withdrew to Miletus, and did not accept
the battle presently offered by the Athenians with one
hundred and eight ships off that port.[4] He awaited a more
favourable opportunity, but the unrest in the allied fleet
continued and increased. Not long before this time the
Athenian fleet had voted the pardon and recall of Alcibiades
at the instigation of Thrasybulus, who himself proceeded to
the Persian headquarters and brought him over to Samos.[5]
On arriving, Alcibiades was elected a colleague of the
Generals. Such was his address that he, the original
proposer of the oligarchic revolution in Athens, was accepted
as a leader by the democrats in the fleet. Further, he
succeeded in conveying the impression that Tissaphernes
also was favourable to the Athenians. This apparent accord
was resented by the allies, and added to the discontent at
Miletus with Astyochus and Tissaphernes. Finally, the
allied fleet broke into open mutiny, and the Milesians seized
the fort built at Miletus by Tissaphernes and expelled the
garrison. The rising was stopped by the opportune arrival
of Mindarus from Lacedæmon to relieve Astyochus, who
went home.[6]

[1] Thu., viii. 82, 86.　　　[2] Ibid., viii. 78.　　　[3] P. 29, *supra.*
[4] Thu., viii. 79.　　　[5] Ibid., viii. 81.　　　[6] Ibid., viii. 83-85.

It will be seen that since the reorganisation of the Athenian fleet and the assumption by Astyochus of the command of the allied fleet, in November 412, the operations at sea had been influenced by those on land, and the military action by land and sea had been deflected by political and economic influences and by personal intrigues, which had all tended to prevent any decision by battle. The result reached was that two nearly equal fleets were massed at Samos and Miletus respectively, thirty sea miles apart, and watched each other. There was a military equilibrium, which was unstable because the political system of the Athenian empire was unstable, but the more immediate cause of its upset at this time was economic. The readiness of Byzantium and other Athenian tributary cities to revolt tempted, and the difficulty in supplying such a large fleet without the help of Tissaphernes, forced the allies to send Clearchus, the son of Ramphias, with forty ships from Miletus to the Hellespont, where Pharnabazus had promised to maintain them. The flanking position of the Athenian fleet at Samos forced Clearchus to pass well to the westward outside that island, instead of making the usual coasting voyage. In consequence his squadron was dispersed by bad weather and was driven to seek shelter at Delos and other places. Only ten ships reached Byzantium, which revolted from Athens on their arrival. Clearchus with the remainder returned to Miletus, whence he himself proceeded overland to the Hellespont. The revolt at Byzantium following that brought about by Dercyllidas at Abydus, some months earlier, threatened the Euxine corn supply to Athens. As soon as the revolt became known at Samos an Athenian detachment was sent to the Hellespont, and an action was fought off Byzantium by eight ships against eight, with results not known.[1]

On assuming command, Mindarus found the allied fleet partially committed to operations in the Hellespont, but held back by the influence of Tissaphernes, who announced his intention to bring up the Phœnician fleet of one hundred and forty-seven ships from Aspendus, a port nearly two hundred miles eastward of Rhodes. He went there, as also did Alcibiades, with thirteen Athenian triremes. Mindarus like-

[1] Thu., viii. 80.

wise sent an officer, Philippus, a Lacedæmonian, with two
triremes to the same place.   About the same time he detached
thirteen triremes under Dorieus to Rhodes to settle some
local question,[1] also sixteen ships to the Hellespont to overrun the Chersonese.   After an interval, Philippus reported
that Tissaphernes had no intention to bring up the Phœnician
fleet, and as his agents at Miletus were withholding supplies
from the fleet, Mindarus decided no longer to act with him,
but to rely on Pharnabazus.[2]   That decision made it necessary
to shift the base from Miletus to the Hellespont, where the
allied fleet would be close to its supplies from Asia and would
flank the Athenian line of supply from the Euxine.   The
Hellespont was the area most favourable to the allies, and
its control was essential to the Athenians.   Like Themistocles
at Salamis, Mindarus was about to force a battle in his own
chosen waters.   His threat to the Euxine corn trade was to
apply the Greek theory of war on land to war at sea.[3]

The dispositions of the fleets at this time seem to have
been as follows :—

	Allied.	Athenian.
In Byzantian waters	8[4]	...
In the Hellespont	16[5]	20[6]
In Lesbian waters	...	5[7]
At Rhodes under Dorieus	13[8]	...
With Philippus or Alcibiades in the south	2[9]	13[10]
At Miletus or Samos	73[11]	60[12]
At Chios or unmanned at Samos	?	9[13]
	112	107

In the operations about to be described we are to remember
that the movements on both sides were limited by difficulties
of food supply, by the need to beach the ships at short
intervals, and by the weather conditions.   It was seemingly
in July 411 that Mindarus, after making every preparation,
started from Miletus for the Hellespont with seventy-three
ships.   His movements indicate an intention to evade the
Athenian fleet, then at Samos, and to avoid battle.   By

[1] Diodorus, xiii. c. 4.   [2] Thu., viii. 85, 87, 88, 99.   [3] P. 47, *supra*.
[4] Thu., viii. 107.   [5] Ibid., viii. 99.   [6] Ibid., viii. 100, 102.
[7] Ibid., viii. 100.   [8] Diodorus, xiii. c. 4.   [9] Thu., viii. 87.
[10] Ibid., viii. 88.   [11] Ibid., viii. 99.   [12] Ibid., viii. 100.
[13] Ibid., viii. 108.

stress of weather he was driven to take shelter at the island of Icaria, forty to fifty sea miles from Miletus, where he stayed five or six days. Thence he proceeded to Chios, distant about forty-five miles, where he remained two whole days to provision his ships.[1]

On hearing that Mindarus had sailed from Miletus, Thrasyllus at once left Samos with fifty-five ships and passed Chios where he sighted the allied fleet. His aim was to bring Mindarus to action, but he also had to cover Lesbos, which was in a state of unrest and disaffected to Athens. Unable either to remain and watch the enemy at Chios, owing to the difficulty of supply, or to proceed to and await him near his destination, the Hellespont, since Lesbos would then be uncovered, he adopted a middle course. Having placed look-outs on the mainland opposite the island of Chios and on the island of Lesbos, to give warning of the enemy's movements, and ordered supplies of food to be collected at Lesbian ports, he coasted along to Methymna, a port on the north coast of the island, about eighty-five sea miles from Chios and forty-three from the Hellespont. There he was well placed, if Mindarus passed east of Lesbos, which, with that island controlled by Athens, was the longer but more favourable route for a rowing fleet requiring shelter from the wind and closely spaced ports of call. He was constrained to leave that position and to proceed thirty-five sea miles to Eresus, a town on the south-west coast which had revolted from Athens. Thus, the call from the land deflected the operations at sea and opened the passage to the Hellespont. At Eresus he found Thrasybulus with five ships from Samos, and was joined by two ships returning from the Hellespont, also by a detachment from Methymna, which raised his numbers to sixty-seven. He prepared to take Eresus.[2]

Less than forty-eight hours after Thrasyllus passed Chios, Mindarus put to sea. He probably sailed at dawn, since the crews had their midday meal at the island of Carteria, distant forty sea miles, and supped at the Arginusæ Islands, distant twenty miles. Sailing next day before dawn, he reached at midday Harmathus, probably Sivriji Bay, on the

---

[1] Thu., viii., 99, 101.   [2] Ibid., viii. 100.

mainland nearly opposite Methymna, distant forty miles, and arrived at Rhœteum and other ports in or near the Hellespont, distant fifty miles, before midnight. In two days the fleet had rowed one hundred and fifty miles at a speed of about five knots.[1]

Warned of the enemy's approach by the beacon·fires lighted by their scouts, the eighteen Athenian ships lying at Sestus started during the night to row the seventeen sea miles down the Hellespont; they passed the sixteen allied ships at Abydus without hindrance, but were too late to clear the entrance under cover of darkness. At dawn they were sighted and chased by Mindarus' fleet. The four ships in the rear were caught: three were driven ashore on the Chersonese and one at Imbros; the rest got away. The squadron from Abydus joined Mindarus, who proceeded to that place after a few hours' blockade of Elæus, a town on the European shore, close to the entrance of the Hellespont. Thrasyllus at Eresus was sixty sea miles away and did not reach Elæus with the Athenian fleet until the following day. On his passage he captured two of the allied ships which had been detached in pursuit of the ships from Sestus. Some of these last now joined him; his strength after their junction is given as seventy-six, and that of Mindarus as eighty-eight.[2]

Thus, in the struggle between the rival political systems of Athens and Lacedæmon, economic necessity, overriding personal intrigue, gradually brought the two fleets into the central strategic area to fight for the money and food without which fleets cannot be maintained. The battle of Cynossema, which seems to have been fought in August 411, resulted in a victory for the Athenians, as has been already related, and was followed by the capture of Cyzicus, an unwalled city on the Asiatic coast of the Propontis.[3]

The full meaning of the victory can only be realised in connection with events in Athens since the overthrow of the democracy by the oligarchist Four Hundred some four or five months earlier. It will be remembered that the fleet at

---

[1] If Mindarus steered south and passed round outside the island of Chios as has been suggested, the time must be increased one day at least, and the distance fifty miles.—Thu., viii. 101.

[2] Ibid., viii. 102-104.   [3] Ibid., viii. 107.

Samos refused to accept the oligarchy. Seeing that Athens depended upon the fleet to cover its oversea food supply, whereas the fleet did not depend upon Athens but drew supplies from elsewhere, it is evident that the fleet was the dominant factor. Its refusal of support undermined the new form of government. The consequent insecurity of the oligarchy encouraged the democratic opposition and drove the oligarchist leaders to make questionable overtures to Lacedæmon.[1] Furthermore, the political strife in Athens tended to encourage revolt in Eubœa, and led the Eubœans to apply to Lacedæmon for aid.[2] In consequence an allied squadron of forty-two triremes under Agesandridas, the son of Agesander, a Spartan, appeared in the Saronic Gulf, overran Ægina, and seemed to threaten with oligarchist connivance an entry into the Piræus. The danger provoked a democratic rising. After a short stay at Epidaurus, Agesandridas advanced along the coast of Salamis, causing great emotion in Athens, passed the Piræus, and rounded the Sunium Promontory to Oropus,[3] which had been betrayed to the Bœotians and lost to Athens some months earlier. There the allied fleet threatened the Athenian hold on Eubœa, which was all-important, seeing that Attica was still overrun by the enemy, and the corn supply from the Euxine was threatened by the revolt of Byzantium. To meet the danger the Athenians hastily manned and sent a fleet of thirty-six ships under Thymochares to Eretria, a harbour about four sea miles from Oropus. On arrival the crews landed to get food. Presently the allied fleet surprised them while many of their men were still absent. With half-manned ships they put to sea, and were totally defeated with a loss of twenty-two triremes. Shortly afterwards all Eubœa, except the important town of Histiæa, revolted from Athens.[4]

Amid these critical conditions, with Attica and Eubœa in the hands of the enemy, no ships to cover the sea supplies of food, and civil discord within their gates, the Athenians were called upon to act. They manned an additional twenty ships, and summoned an assembly which displaced the oligarchy and substituted a democratic form of government, voted the

[1] Thu., viii. 90.   [2] Ibid., viii. 91.
[3] Ibid., viii. 92-95.   [4] Ibid., viii. 95.

recall of Alcibiades and other exiles, and sent to the fleet a message encouraging vigorous action.[1]　Shortly afterwards the news of the victory at Cynossema reached Athens.　The stress in home waters was at once relieved, since the allies were forced to concentrate and to send reinforcements to the Hellespont.

Mindarus called up all the allied ships—fifty in number—from Eubœa, but only a few joined him, as the greater number were wrecked in rounding the iron-bound Acte (Athos) Peninsula.[2]　Athens countered with a small reinforcement under Thymochares.　A second indecisive battle followed in the Hellespont.　Shortly afterwards—say in October—Dorieus with fourteen allied ships, and Alcibiades with eighteen Athenian ships from the south, joined the main fleets.　A third battle was fought near Abydus and resulted in the defeat of the allies, who lost thirty ships.[3]

After the battle the allies withdrew to Abydus, where they were covered by, and acted in conjunction with, the army of Pharnabazus; the Athenians fell back on Sestus, where they had no such support.　The allies remained concentrated, their supplies being assured by Pharnabazus, who controlled the wealth of that part of Asia.　The Athenians dispersed to collect money from the cities of the Ægean, the detachments from the fleet being supplemented by an additional squadron of thirty ships under Theramenes, the Athenian, at the instance of Thrasyllus, who returned to Athens.　Only forty ships remained together at Sestus.[4]　As a consequence, when Mindarus threatened an attack with sixty ships the Athenians were compelled to withdraw to Cardia, a port on the west side of the Chersonese.[5]　Thus the allies were left in control of the Hellespont and Propontis, and free about the vernal equinox in the year 410 to make a combined attack by land and sea on Cyzicus, which they captured.[6]　As a counter-stroke the Athenians concentrated upwards of eighty ships from all parts of the Ægean under the command of Alcibiades, Thrasybulus, and Theramenes, passed up the Hellespont, entered the Propontis, fell upon and destroyed or captured the whole allied fleet of at least sixty ships.　Mindarus him-

[1] Thu., viii. 97.　　　[2] Diodorus, xiii. c. 4.　　　[3] Xen., *Hell.*, I. i. 6, 7.
[4] Ibid., I. i. 8.　　　[5] Ibid., I. i. 11.　　　[6] Ibid., I. i. 13.

self was among the slain.[1] Athens was again supreme at sea, but the army of Lacedæmon was still undefeated, over-ran Attica, and threatened Athens.

According to Diodorus, Lacedæmon now made overtures for peace on the basis of a retention of cities captured by either side, a withdrawal of garrisons—*e.g.*, from Pylus and Deceleia, and an exchange of prisoners. A peace on such terms could be only an armed truce, so long as the decision between the armed forces remained incomplete and the rival political systems continued at issue. Athens rejected the overtures.[2] During this and the following years she made no attempt to reach the decision on land essential to her security. All her efforts were directed to secure food from the Euxine to feed her citizens, and money from her sometime tributary cities to maintain her fleets. By the force of circumstances she was compelled to pursue secondary aims. To follow these in detail is unnecessary. It will suffice to say that, shortly after the battle of Cyzicus, the Athenians advanced into the Propontis, levied contributions on certain cities, and occupied others. They then seized and fortified Chrysopolis, a position in the Bosporus opposite Byzantium. This done, the main fleet withdrew to the Hellespont, leaving a squadron of thirty ships to protect the trade out of the Euxine, on which they levied tolls.[3] The corn supply to Athens from the Euxine, which had probably been interrupted by the revolt of Byzantium and Abydus during the previous year, was now reopened, and Eubœa being hostile, the port of Thoricus on the east coast of Attica was fortified to afford protection to the corn ships.[4] To stop this trade, which largely neutralised the effect produced by the occupation of Attica, the allies sent Clearchus towards the close of the year with a squadron of fifteen ships to Byzantium. With the loss of three ships he passed the nine Athenian guard-ships in the Hellespont, reached his destination, and may have added to the Athenian difficulties of convoy through the Bosporus.[5]

In the year 409 the only operations of moment seem to have been an expedition of fifty triremes accompanied by a land force under Thrasyllus, who left Athens in the summer

---

[1] Xen., *Hell.*, I. i. 13, 18. [2] Diodorus, xiii. 6. [3] Xen., *Hell.*, I. i. 20, 22.
[4] Ibid., I. ii. 1. [5] Ibid., I. i. 36.

for Samos, and thence raided the neighbouring mainland cities for money and slaves. After some initial successes he was defeated at Ephesus by the townsmen, aided by a force under Tissaphernes, and by the crews of a Syracusan squadron of twenty-five ships.[1] Forced to re-embark, he proceeded to Mitylene in Lesbos, whence he issued to intercept the aforesaid Syracusan squadron, which he chased back to Ephesus, capturing four ships. He then joined the main fleet under Alcibiades in the Hellespont. Their united forces occupied Lampsacus, failed to take Abydus, and plundered the surrounding country during the winter.[2]

In the following spring, 408, the whole Athenian armament moved against Chalcedon. After a protracted siege and the defeat of an attempted relief by Pharnabazus, the city agreed to pay tribute, including all arrears, and Pharnabazus undertook to hand over a lump sum of money, and to conduct an Athenian embassy to the Great King.[3] Furthermore, a truce was arranged between the Athenians and Pharnabazus until the return of the embassy. Siege was now laid to Byzantium, which towards the winter was betrayed into the hands of the besiegers.[4]

These successes secured to Athens the safety of the Euxine corn trade and the tribute from the Hellespontine region, while the truce relieved the territory of Pharnabazus from further raids. The Athenians, unable to plunder that area, and always in want of money to maintain the fleet, transferred their armament to the Ægean during the winter 408-7. Alcibiades with twenty ships levied contributions from the cities in Caria; Thrasybulus with thirty ships subdued Thasus and the revolted cities in Thrace; Thrasyllus returned to Athens with the remainder of the fleet. Enriched with the wealth exacted from captured or tributary cities, Alcibiades afterwards crossed the Ægean from Samos, touching at Paros, to the Laconian Gulf, looked into Gythium, where Lacedæmon was reported to be fitting out thirty ships, and is said to have reached Athens in May 407.[5] Before the return of Thrasyllus

---

[1] Xen., *Hell.*, I. ii. 1-9.   [2] Ibid., I. ii. 12, 14, 17.
[3] Ibid., I. iii. 2, 5, 8.   [4] Ibid., I. iii. 14, 16, 20.
[5] Ibid., I. iv. 8, 9, 11, 12. There is a difference of opinion among scholars as to the year of Alcibiades' return. The dates in the text are derived from Grote and Beloch; those of Curtius are one year earlier.

he had been elected one of the Generals, his colleagues being Thrasybulus and Conon; now he was given the absolute command of all the forces. His offences against the State were condoned in view of his recent services. He was at the summit of his career, but a change was at hand.[1]

Early in the year 407, the Athenian embassy,[2] accompanied by Pharnabazus, was met on its way to Susa by Cyrus the Younger, the second son of Darius, who was about to assume the government of a large part of Asia Minor and the control of the war. The envoys were stopped and interned by his orders, thus destroying whatever hopes the Athenians may have held of coming to terms with the Great King, or of detaching him from the cause of the allies.[3] Cyrus seems to have reached Sardes not long after the vernal equinox, and to have been joined there shortly afterwards by Lysander the Spartan, who had assumed command of the allied fleet about the new year. The Admiral had taken the southern route *viâ* Rhodes, Cos, and Miletus to Ephesus, where his line of advance to the Hellespont was not flanked from Samos, and he was near to Sardes. At Ephesus he had collected some seventy triremes, the product of the efforts made by his predecessors, aided by Pharnabazus, to rebuild the fleet during the three years following the defeat of Cyzicus. Aided by liberal subsidies from Cyrus, he raised the pay of the fleet personnel, making good the arrears; he also gradually improved the equipment of the ships and the organisation of the fleet, which by the autumn had grown to ninety ships.[4]

Meanwhile Alcibiades had been given a force of one hundred triremes, together with a landing force of fifteen hundred heavy armed infantry, and one hundred and fifty horse. Leaving Athens early in September, he disembarked near Gaurium in Andros, which had revolted from Athens, and, with Euboea hostile, was doubtless a base dangerous to her trade with the Hellespont. After a stay of three days, during which the Andrians were driven within their walls, he sailed for Samos, leaving Conon with twenty ships to besiege Gaurium.[5] The two fleets, about equal in number, were

---

[1] Xen., *Hell.*, I. iv. 10, 20.   [2] P. 100, *supra*.   [3] Xen., *Hell.*, I. iv. 2, 6.
[4] Ibid., I. v. 1, 2, 7, 10.   [5] Ibid., I. iv. 21, 22; v. 18.

H

now face to face at Ephesus and Samos, twenty-five sea miles apart. There was equilibrium, but time was on the side of the allies, since their supply and maintenance were assured by Cyrus, who controlled the wealth of Asia, whereas the Athenians were dependent upon such contributions of money and food as they could wring from the cities on the Ægean. Athens produced nothing, and had long since expended her accumulated wealth. Lysander remained concentrated, and awaited a more favourable opportunity, which was not long in coming.

Whether impatient of inaction, or elated by past success, or pressed by difficulties of supply, Alcibiades now divided the fleet. He seems to have moved to Notium, a port some ten miles north-west of Ephesus, and flanking Lysander's line of advance to the Hellespont. There he left the main body in charge of his follower, the pilot Antiochus, a man skilled as a seaman but not as a military leader, and therefore unfit to command. To him were given instructions not to bring on a battle.[1] Alcibiades himself with a detachment proceeded to Phocæa to meet Thrasybulus, who had gone there from the Hellespont and was fortifying that city, seemingly as a base from which to plunder that part of the country. He next made an unprovoked attack on Cymè, a dependent ally of Athens, and plundered its territory.[2] Meanwhile Antiochus, contrary to his instructions, paraded with a small force before the allied fleet at Ephesus, thus defying Lysander to fight. The result was a desultory engagement between a few ships, which developed into a general action. Antiochus, whose ships joined the battle successively and in disorder, was defeated with the loss of fifteen triremes by Lysander, whose fleet was in regular order. Antiochus was among the slain. Alcibiades at once rejoined the defeated fleet, concentrated at Samos, and presently offered battle off Ephesus, but Lysander did not move.[3]

The defeat, coupled with the errors in judgment from which it resulted, having destroyed the prestige of Alcibiades both in the fleet and at Athens, he was superseded and withdrew with one trireme to his estate in the Chersonese. Ten other

[1] Xen., *Hell.*, I. v. 11, 12.   [2] Diodorus, xiii. 9.
[3] Xen., *Hell.*, I. v. 13, 14, 15.

generals were chosen, of whom the chief was Conon. That officer was relieved at Andros and ordered to Samos with his squadron. On his arrival the fleet was reorganised and found to number seventy effective ships. The money and food for its maintenance during the following months were found by plundering the enemy's coasts.[1]

It was now December 407. According to the custom of Lacedæmon, Lysander had been relieved at the end of his year of command by Callicratidas, who found himself criticised as unversed in naval affairs and opposed not only by the followers of Lysander in the fleet and by oligarchic factions in the littoral cities of Ionia, but also by Cyrus, who refused to receive him when he went to Sardes. Furthermore, he was without money to pay and maintain the fleet, as Lysander had returned to Cyrus such part of the subsidy as was unexpended, and no fresh grant was forthcoming. The opposition in the fleet was disarmed by a tactful appeal to the Lacedæmonians. The rebuff given by Cyrus was met by the transfer of the fleet from Ephesus to Miletus[2] and by an appeal to the Milesians for financial aid, which they gave. Meanwhile he manned fifty additional ships from Chios, Rhodes, and other cities, thus raising his number to one hundred and forty triremes.[3] With this force Callicratidas put to sea from Miletus in the spring of 406, and seems to have called at Chios, where he received from the Chians some money which helped to pay his crews. Thence sailing northward, he is said to have detached one or two littoral cities from the Athenian interest. Finally, he reached Methymna in Lesbos, then held by an Athenian garrison, and carried the city by storm after suffering a first repulse. The city was plundered and the captured slaves sold, but the Greek captives were set free, in those days an unprecedented act, which showed the Pan-Hellenic sympathies of Callicratidas.[4]

Meanwhile, Conon with seventy ships, anxious to make a diversion to relieve Methymna, arrived at the Hekatonnêsi Islands, some twenty sea miles to the eastward. When putting to sea after the fall of Methymna, he was attacked at

---

[1] Xen., *Hell.*, I. v. 16, 17, 18, 20.   [2] Ibid., I. vi. 1, 4, 5, 6, 7.
[3] Ibid., I. vi. 3.   [4] Ibid., I. vi. 12, 13, 14.

daybreak by Callicratidas, who had left that port during the night with one hundred and seventy ships. With the loss of thirty ships Conon reached Mitylene, hauled up his ships under the walls, and was there closely blockaded by land and sea.[1] Provisions being short and relief necessary, two fast-rowing triremes attempted to run the blockade. One of these was captured; the other got through with the news to Athens, and also found means to send word to Diomedon at Samos. The latter tried to communicate with Conon through the Euripus (Port Iero), but ten out of his twelve ships were taken, Diomedon with two ships escaping with difficulty.[2] As soon as the news reached Athens one hundred and ten triremes were ordered to be manned, and all men of military age, both freemen and slaves, were compelled to go on board, the latter being promised manumission in the event of success. Thirty days later the fleet was ready and sailed for Samos, where ten Samian and thirty allied triremes joined, thus raising the force to one hundred and fifty,[3] with crews exceeding thirty thousand in number. The whole fleet then proceeded to the Arginusæ Islands, distant twelve sea miles from Mitylene. It was now August. On hearing of the enemy's approach, Callicratidas left Eteonicus with fifty ships to contain the forty under Conon, and with the other hundred and twenty, with crews of about twenty-five thousand, moved to Malea, six miles south of Mitylene. There they took their evening meal, and, after the sun went down, saw the Athenian watch-fires at the Arginusæ Islands eight miles to the east.[4] On the following day the Athenians won a complete victory—as has been already related[5]—and destroyed two-thirds of the allied fleet with a loss to themselves of only twenty-five ships. Callicratidas was among those drowned. After the battle the remnant of the allied fleet fled to Chios and Phocæa; the Athenians returned to the Arginusæ Islands without attempting to rescue the unfortunate crews of their own crippled ships.[6] Whether this omission was due to bad weather, as alleged, or to unpardonable neglect arising out of a divided responsibility, or to some other cause, the loss of so many—

[1] Xen., *Hell.*, I. vi. 15, 17, 18.
[2] Ibid., I. vi. 19, 21, 22, 23.
[3] Ibid., I. vi. 24, 25.
[4] Ibid., I. vi. 26, 27, 28.
[5] P. 42, *supra.*
[6] Ibid., I. vi. 33, 34, 35.

perhaps one thousand—lives, without any apparent attempt to rescue them, was bitterly resented by their fellow-country-men at home. All the admirals present in the battle were recalled, condemned without any proper trial, and six were executed.[1]

As soon as the news of the defeat reached Eteonicus, he raised the blockade of Mitylene and withdrew with the land force to Methymna, while the triremes and merchant ships ran for Chios before a strong favourable wind, which sprang up after the battle. The same strong wind drove the Athenians back to their anchorage at the Arginusæ Islands and detained them there until the following morning, when they put to sea and joined Conon, who then issued from Mitylene. After a futile attempt on Chios the Athenians returned to Samos.[2]

Athens was again supreme at sea, but the Lacedæmonian army was still undefeated. A firm peace could only come from a double decision on land and sea in favour of one side. Athens was unable to raise an army strong enough to reach a decision on land, and could only maintain her fleet by means of exactions from the littoral cities of the Ægean. The allies could still hope to win a decision at sea, since their man power was backed by the wealth of Asia, which remained available for the construction and maintenance of a fleet.

These being the conditions, ambassadors from an allied assembly at Ephesus, accompanied by messengers from Cyrus, were sent to Lacedæmon, requesting that Lysander might again be sent to Ionia. The request was granted, but to evade the law which forbade any man holding the office more than once, they appointed a certain Aracus as admiral, and made Lysander his nominal subordinate but the real commander.[3] On arrival at Ephesus about the opening of the year 405, Lysander at once began to concentrate and refit all available ships and to build others. He was financed by Cyrus, who not only gave him such money as he could then spare, but, when summoned to attend Darius in Media, assigned to Lysander the government and the entire revenues of the satrapy.[4] Thus amply provided with money, he was

---

[1] Xen., *Hell.*, I. vii. 34.
[2] Ibid., I. vi. 37, 38.
[3] Ibid., II. i. 6, 7.
[4] Ibid., II. i. 10, 11, 14.

able to put to sea in the spring with a large fleet fully manned and equipped. For reasons not disclosed, he did not seek a battle at this time, but proceeded south to Caria, passed to Rhodes, and thence seems to have worked his way to the coast of Attica. He did not remain there, but, not long before the autumnal equinox, passed on to the Hellespont to force the battle he wanted in the waters most favourable to himself.[1]

Meanwhile the Athenians were possibly fettered in their movements by difficulties of supply and did not follow Lysander, but remained near Samos, plundering Chios and the neighbouring cities in Asia. On hearing that Lysander was besieging Lampsacus in the Hellespont, they proceeded for that place, and on the morning following their arrival at Elæus in the Chersonese, learnt that the city had fallen.[2] Without delay they proceeded to Sestus, whence after provisioning they passed on and arrived the same evening at Ægospotami, an open beach on the European shore, ten sea miles above Sestus and from two to four below Lampsacus, which is in Asia.[3] The Athenian fleet numbered one hundred and eighty ships, manned by upwards of thirty-six thousand men, and was commanded by Conon and five other admirals; Lysander had one hundred and seventy ships with upwards of thirty-four thousand men. The Athenians drew their supplies from distant Sestus, the allies from Lampsacus close at hand. On the morrow before daybreak Lysander gave his crews breakfast, manned his ships and prepared for battle, but gave strict orders that no ship was to move. The Athenians manned their ships, formed up, and offered battle, but refrained from attack. Later in the day, seeing no chance of a battle, they withdrew to Ægospotami, landed, and scattered to procure and cook their food. Thus, they left their unmanned ships liable to a surprise attack by a fleet fully manned and prepared for battle less than thirty minutes distant. Lysander, recognising the danger, kept the ships manned until he was certain that the Athenian crews had landed and dispersed. On four consecutive days the Athenians offered battle, withdrew, and landed, while Lysander stood

---

[1] Xen., *Hell.*, II. i. 15, 17 ; Diodorus, xiii. 15.   [2] Xen., *Hell.*, II. i. 16, 20.
[3] Ibid., II. i. 20, 21.

prepared but remained unmoved.[1] Alcibiades, who was in the neighbourhood and watched events, is said to have warned the Athenian admirals of their danger. No heed was paid to his warning.[2] This is the more remarkable, seeing that the conditions were similar to those which had led to the defeat of the Athenians under Thymochares off Eretria in the year 411. On the fifth day, as soon as the Athenians had landed and dispersed, Lysander fell on them in their defenceless state, and with very small loss captured or destroyed the whole fleet, except nine ships, which escaped under Conon.[3]

The Athenian defeat was due neither to numbers nor to weapons, nor to tactical skill, but to neglect of ordinary precautions, whether brought about by incompetence or treachery is not known. Since the Lacedæmonian army was supreme on land and was at the gates of Athens, the destruction of her fleet at Ægospotami was the double decision which disarmed Athens. She was deprived of all her dependencies, and after a prolonged blockade by land and sea was starved into submission and unconditional surrender some ten months later, or about the vernal equinox 404. Thus the commercial blockade derived from the battle only became effective after the primary military aim had been achieved.

[1] Xen., *Hell.*, II. i. 22, 23, 24. [2] Ibid., II. i. 25, 26.
[3] Ibid., II. i. 27, 28, 29.

X.

SUMMARY AND CONCLUSION.

It will be useful to recapitulate shortly, and to emphasise the chief points in which ancient practice illustrates modern theory. In the wars under review, the political object is seen to be political dominance on the one side and security on the other. But Athens changes her rôle. In the Persian war she seeks security, in the Peloponnesian her aim is to dominate. The economic influence is prominent in the Peloponnesian war. The supply of food, the tribute to Athens, and the Persian subsidies are clearly seen to affect largely the military operations.

That war culminates in battle, and that the destruction of the armed force is the decisive act, is evident from the results of the double decision at Salamis and Platæa, and by the single one at Ægospotami. In each case the political object was attained through victory. The war in Ionia supplies examples of the fleets in equilibrium, their action being reciprocally neutralised, as when they faced each other at Miletus and Samos. The Persian war showed the sea battle of Salamis and the land battle of Platæa as independent tactical activities. The Syracusan expedition ended in disaster, mainly because the Athenian navy was used so largely to supplement the army in land operations that its efficiency was gradually undermined, and its destruction resulted. The true interdependence of the fleet and army is well brought out in the campaign of Salamis, when decisions, with their corresponding mutual reactions, were reached by each on its own element.

The same operations mark the need for the double decision

by land and sea, as is also evident from the Peloponnesian war. During the ten years' war the Athenian navy was supreme, and after the disaster at Syracuse again became so in consequence of the victories of Cyzicus and Arginusæ. Nevertheless, no final result followed, because in each case the Lacedæmonian army remained undefeated. On the other hand, Ægospotami gave the double decision required to end the war, since that army was already supreme on land. This need for a double decision shows that a navy is not of itself a menace to the independence of a Continental power, and accounts for its importance as the supplement to an army in a Continental war—*e.g.*, the British Navy.

In the evolution of the battle is to be noted the ephemeral existence of the "new system" of tactics, which depended chiefly on superior speed and skill in handling individual ships. Means were found to neutralise these by a choice of site for the battle unfavourable to them. Finally, they disappeared, and "the law of equality" asserted itself. The later battles were won not by petty, trifling manœuvres, but by skill in throwing masses of ships into battle, and by hard fighting. Arginusæ was the prototype of Trafalgar.

The flanking position used by Themistocles, and recommended by Hermocrates to limit the movements of a hostile fleet, remains the chief foundation on which rests all strategy at sea. For more than three centuries the defence of this country from invasion has been based upon it, the detachments of small ships holding the Channel and the narrow seas being covered from an enemy advancing in force out of the Atlantic by the main fleet based on a western port— *e.g.*, Plymouth or Torbay. The same principle might have been applied in the North Sea during the war with Germany, since a fleet in the Forth would have covered the detachments holding the Straits of Dover and the northern exits.

The influence of man is seen collectively in the difference between the skilled crews of the Athenians and the untrained levies opposed to them, and individually in the contrast between Themistocles and Alcibiades, or between Lysander and Nicias, also in the parts played by Demosthenes and Brasidas. Until these men had been tried their fitness for command remained uncertain, and even after that the reciprocal reaction of the leaders on either side was equally so.

The first ten years of the Peloponnesian war is peculiarly instructive in the light thrown on the secondary results. These became prominent in the absence of the double decision, which could not be obtained, because the armed force was a navy on the one side and an army on the other. The attempt of the Athenians to stop the trade of the Peloponnesus, and of the Peloponnesians to intercept the tribute by detaching the tributary cities from Athens, resulted only in a peace by agreement which satisfied no one. Subsequent experience has tended to confirm the conclusion that a political object of fundamental importance can only be attained by a military decision. No economic pressure short of total inability to resist due to starvation will force men to yield when their existence is at stake and their passions are roused, as was shown by the example of Athens, and confirmed by numerous later instances.

INDEX.